Wild Mushrooms and Other Very Short Stories

Jake Allsop

PENGUIN BOOKS

PENGUIN BOOKS

Published by the Penguin Group
Penguin Books Ltd, 27 Wrights Lane, London W8 5TZ, England
Penguin Books USA Inc., 375 Hudson Street, New York, New York 10014, USA
Penguin Books Australia Ltd, Ringwood, Victoria, Australia
Penguin Books Canada Ltd, 10 Alcorn Avenue, Toronto, Ontario, Canada M4V 3B2
Penguin Books (NZ) Ltd, 182–190 Wairau Road, Auckland 10, New Zealand

Penguin Books Ltd, Registered Offices: Harmondsworth, Middlesex, England

First published 1989
1 3 5 7 9 10 8 6 4 2

Printed in England by Clays Ltd, St Ives plc
Set in Linotron 202 Plantin

Contents

Introduction

After the grammar and the exercises and the conversation practice, what do we language learners do? We read. Reading is a way of (a) strengthening what we already know; (b) increasing our vocabulary; (c) feeling that we are making good use of our time in trains, buses, coffee bars and bed.

The trouble is that people tell us to read newspapers (often very difficult); or novels (too long); or works of literature (too heavy for our purposes). And there is something else: if you read something because you feel you ought to read it, but you are not really interested in it, you end up feeling guilty or sad or angry. So, for us simple language learners, it would be nice to find something to read which is:

- worth reading anyway, that is, we would enjoy reading it even if it were in our own language;
- in small, bite-sized pieces – snacks rather than seven-course meals – that we could finish at a single sitting;
- full of useful and usable language, idioms and everyday expressions;
- accompanied by a few painless explanations, and a bit of language practice which helps to fix new language items in our minds.

I think it would be very difficult to write a book which satisfied all these requirements, but I have tried, in these Very Short Stories, to do so. The stories are set in a variety of locations:

not only England and Europe, but also as far afield as Africa and Australia. They are all, in one way or another, about people and – my main obsession – about what makes people tick.

The language practice makes use of the many idiomatic expressions used in the text. No key to the exercises is given: you should go back to the text to find the original expressions.

I hope that you enjoy the stories, and that, along the way, you improve your English.

Mangiarotti

Date-line: Paris, July, 1960, as the TV reporters say. I was twenty years old, and I was starving to death. I hadn't eaten anything for two days, except for half a cheese sandwich that I found in the lining of my coat: I remember eating the first half in late May of the same year. It had taken me a week to hitch-hike to Paris from Italy, and my money had run out. Before I left Milan, my friend Silvano had told me that he knew a man in Paris who might be able to give me a job. The man's name was Mangiarotti – he didn't seem to have a first name – and he was a painter. Mangiarotti worked somewhere in the 14th *arrondissement*, the Porte de Vanves area of Paris. Now, to say that you are a painter in Paris sounds quite romantic, so perhaps I should add that he was not an artist but a house-painter. According to Silvano, Mangiarotti specialised in painting shop fronts.

Anyway, as soon as I arrived in Paris I spent my last few centimes on a Metro ride to Plaisance, which seemed to be right in the middle of the 14th *arrondissement*, and started to wander through the streets searching for anyone who looked like an Italian house-painter. I searched high and low, tramping along main streets, peering down side streets, asking passers-by, poking my head into every baker's and greengrocer's and fish-monger's as I went; but in vain. No sign of Mangiarotti.

By the end of the first day, I was so desperate that I sold my watch to a second-hand dealer – funny how my expensive Timex

3

was suddenly worth little more than the price of an omelette and chips. That night, I slept on a hard bench in the local park. I woke next morning stiff and cold and as hungry as ever. I'd better get up and start looking for Mangiarotti, I thought.
30 Mangiarotti? I didn't even know what he looked like, for goodness' sake! I imagined a short, dark-haired, sun-tanned man – in other words, the typical Englishman's idea of the typical Italian. But what if he were tall, red-haired and fair-skinned? I had seen Italians from the Alto Adige who looked like that.
35 Talk about looking for a needle in a haystack! All the same, there was nothing for it but to continue the search.

Finally, towards the end of the afternoon, when my feet ached and my shoulder hurt from the weight of my bag and my empty stomach groaned with hunger, my luck changed. I happened to
40 look down a side street and saw, to my delight, a man up a ladder, paintbrush in hand. As I approached, I saw that he was short, dark-haired and sun-tanned: the typical Englishman's idea of the typical Italian! Moreover, he was painting the front of a shop. I called up to him.

45 '*Scusi, signore.* Excuse me,' I said in my best Italian. 'Are you Mr Mangiarotti?'

He came down the ladder and eyed me silently while he wiped the paint from his brush with an old rag. His stare made me feel uncomfortable, for it seemed to go straight through me. He
50 continued to look me up and down without speaking. I felt stupid, so I went on:

'I am a friend of Silvano Agosto, and he told me that . . .' My words trailed off into silence as he turned away from me to put his paintbrush down. Then he turned to face me again. I
55 repeated my original question: 'Are you Mr Mangiarotti?' He shrugged his shoulders as if to say that it didn't matter whether he was or not.

Suddenly he addressed me in French: '*Allons boire un coup.* Let's go and have something to drink.'

60 I followed him into a nearby café, where he ordered a glass

4

of a colourless liquid which turned milky when he added water to it. I asked if I could have a white coffee, thinking to myself that the milk in it might do something to satisfy my hunger.

'*Allora, sei un amico di Silvano*. So, you're a friend of Silvano,' he said, switching to Italian without warning.

I nodded.

'*Alors, qu'est-ce que tu fais ici?* So, what are you doing here?' he asked, switching back to French. Why on earth did he keep changing from one language to the other? Was he showing off? Was he making fun of me? Was he just testing me? I felt very confused and uncertain, the way I used to feel in front of a particularly difficult teacher when I was at school. I started to mumble a reply in French, a language that I was not very good at. I explained, as best as I could, that I had been working in Milan, but had decided to spend the summer in Paris, providing, that is, that I could find work.

'Why are you speaking to me in French?' he asked, interrupting me. Then, before I could reply, he roared with laughter. He found the joke – whatever it was – very funny. Suspecting that he was laughing at me, I began to feel more and more irritated. His laughter ceased as suddenly as it had begun. 'Well now, my young friend,' he said, addressing me this time in fluent English, 'you are a friend of Silvano Agosto, you are looking for a Mr Mangiarotti, and you want a job, hmm?' Seeing the look of astonishment on my face at being addressed in English, he added: 'You do speak English, don't you?'

'Of course I do.' I replied angrily. 'I *am* English.'

'I would never have guessed!' he said, and once again burst out laughing. There was an unmistakable tone of irony in his voice.

'How did you know I was English?' I asked, my face still showing anger.

'Oh, come on, my young English friend. Don't look so upset. I was only pulling your leg. It is not so difficult to guess your nationality.'

'How?' I asked. At the tender age of twenty, I liked to think of myself as a citizen of the world, not a typical product of my native country.

'Well, first of all, you are tall and fair-haired. How many Italians are tall and fair? Next, you have a pale complexion, even though you have been living in Italy, the land of sunshine. And your hair-style – forgive me, I do not mean to be rude – could only be English.'

My hair was wavy, long, falling across my forehead, and I had a parting on the left. Was this so typically English? Perhaps he was right.

'As for your shoes . . . !' He did not finish the sentence. I looked down at my feet. Nothing wrong with them, I thought. But, on the other hand, perhaps they were rather traditional in design.

'Finally, my young friend, there is the matter of your Italian. You speak it fluently and quite accurately, it is true. But your accent . . . ! Only an Englishman could pronounce my name the way you do. "Manjer-rottee". Ugh! You make it sound like the name of a fat old horse.'

Despite the rather uncomplimentary things he had said about my appearance and my Italian accent, I couldn't help admiring the way he had worked out my nationality from the various clues. Just like the famous detective, Sherlock Holmes, who could tell from the slightest clue – a cigarette-end perhaps – that the man who had been smoking it was a short, left-handed Turkish watchmaker with a bad cold.

Anyway, the upshot was that Mangiarotti gave me a job, and I settled down in Paris. About two weeks after I had started working for him, I used a few francs to telephone Silvano. After all, it was thanks to Silvano that I had a job in Paris, and I wanted him to know that everything had turned out well.

'Hello, Silvano! It's me! Joe. I'm phoning from Paris. I . . . '

6

Before I could say another word, Silvano interrupted in his   130
usual enthusiastic manner and took over the conversation.

'Hi, Joe! How are you? Everything OK? So you got to Paris,
after all, eh? Good for you! Oh, that reminds me, Joe. You
remember I told you about an Italian that I knew in Paris, a guy
called Mangiarotti. Well, I phoned him the day you left Milan.   135
I described you to him in detail, in case you tried to get in touch
with him. So, he's sort of half-expecting you, Joe. Why don't
you see if you can find him? Or perhaps you have already found
him.'

Oh yes, I had found him all right, Mr Clever Sherlock   140
Holmes Mangiarotti.

The Invisible Man

One day, not long after I had started working for him, Mangiarotti said: 'That's enough work for today. Clear up, will you? I'll be back in ten minutes.' It was typical of him to spring surprises on people, to do things without warning or explanation. I cleaned the paintbrushes carefully, knowing that Mangiarotti would make a fuss if even one tiny speck of paint remained on them. I wasn't scared of him exactly, but he was a man with a sharp tongue, and I tried not to upset him. I packed everything away in the proper, Mangiarotti order: ladders on the left, buckets on the right, and so on.

After about quarter of an hour a car pulled up, and there was Mangiarotti, at the steering-wheel of an old black Citroën. His face was gloomy as usual.

'Get in!' he said. The car pulled away quickly with a squeal of tyres before I'd hardly had a chance to close the door.

'Where are we going?' I asked.

He did not reply, which was his way of telling me to mind my own business. I decided to settle back and enjoy what I could of the ride – after all, it was better than standing on a ladder painting shop fronts. I hadn't the slightest idea where we were going, but we were soon out of Paris and in open countryside. With typical suddenness, Mangiarotti screeched to a stop by the roadside and switched off the engine. I looked at him. He was staring straight ahead. I followed his gaze, but all

9

25 I could see was a country road with a hedge running alongside it.

A movement on the grass verge caught my eye. It was a hat, an old black Homburg, the sort that businessmen used to wear, and it appeared to be alive. It moved forward, stopped, disap-
30 peared, bobbed up again for a second, then moved forward and disappeared again. It was such a ridiculous sight that I burst out laughing, but Mangiarotti, who was also watching the hat, remained serious-faced.

As I turned again to look, it rose up a couple of inches,
35 revealing that there was a head underneath. It dawned on me that there was a ditch between the grass verge and the hedge, and that the wearer of the hat was down in the ditch. Mangi-arotti got out of the car, and walked towards the mysterious hat. I didn't know whether I was supposed to follow him or to stay
40 in the car. My curiosity got the better of me, so I got out and hurried to catch up with him. He stood by the roadside, staring down at the hat and talking brusquely to it in an Italian dialect which I could not understand. I looked down too, and saw, under the hat, the red, wrinkled face of an old man. Despite
45 the hot summer's afternoon, he was wearing a black fur-collared overcoat which perfectly matched his ancient Homburg. The amazing thing was that, although he was standing upright, his head barely cleared the top of the ditch. He was a dwarf of a man, and his small stature was exaggerated by the bent body
50 of old age.

Mangiarotti held out his hand to the old man and pulled him out of the ditch, lifting him momentarily off his feet as if he were a straw doll. I could see now that the old man was not much more than a metre tall. He was clutching a huge briefcase
55 under his arm, which made him seem even smaller. Like his hat and his overcoat, the briefcase was black, and, also like them, had seen better days. I wondered who on earth he was, and what on earth he had been doing in the ditch. Mangiarotti, typically, gave me no explanation, and indeed did not even introduce me

to the old man. The latter tapped the side of his nose and   60
winked at me a couple of times as we walked back to the car,
as if he and I shared a secret. Mangiarotti was holding him by
the arm, but not affectionately. It was more like the grip that
policemen use when they are arresting a wrongdoer. He bundled
the little fellow into the back of the car, and nodded to me to   65
get in.

We drove off with the usual squeal of tyres. The old man was
silent at first. Then he spoke to me: '*Allora, giovanotto . . .* Well,
young man . . .' he said, addressing me in good Italian. I waited
for the rest of the sentence, but nothing came, so I turned round   70
to look at him. Once more, he winked at me and tapped the side
of his nose with his bony forefinger. 'So, *giovanotto*, what do you
think?'

Before I could think of a suitable reply to this baffling question, Mangiarotti uttered a short '*Sta zitto, buffone!* Shut up, you   75
old fool!' to the old man. The old man stuck out his tongue at
the back of Mangiarotti's head. Then he patted his briefcase,
continuing to smile and wink and tap his nose. The expression
on his face suggested that he had the Crown Jewels in there. For
a moment, the thought crossed my mind that he might indeed   80
be some kind of criminal, a burglar perhaps. With his small
stature, he could easily climb in and out of windows, and he
looked very fit and agile despite his years. Perhaps his briefcase
was stuffed with stolen goods.

We arrived back at Mangiarotti's flat in the Rue Blanche   85
towards dusk. He dropped me and the old man off while he
went to park the car. The old man seemed quite agitated, a
mixture of excitement and apprehension.

'Who are you?' he asked me suddenly. It was a fair question,
I suppose, the same question that I was dying to ask him.   90

'I work for Signor Mangiarotti.'

He laughed out loud. '*Signor* Mangiarotti! *Signor* Mangiarotti!' he shouted. 'That —! He is no *signore!* He is a —!' I did
not know the words he used, but their meaning was clear: he

95 had a very low opinion of my employer. 'But, don't you worry, *giovanotto*. I'll be ready soon, and then I'll show *Signor* Mangiarotti a thing or two . . . I'll be rid of him for ever!' He patted his briefcase again, and gave a little jump, the sort of spring that you associate with elves or fairies. He was for all the world like

100 an elf at that moment, a tiny being full of magic and mischief. I decided that I liked him, even though I was quite sure that he was as mad as a hatter. 'I'll show you later,' he whispered, 'when *he*'s not around. Our secret, *giovanotto*. *Vabbene?* OK?' He winked and tapped the side of his nose again.

105 '*Vabbene*,' I replied, humouring him.

Mangiarotti returned a moment later, his face blacker than ever, probably because he had had difficulty in finding a parking space. We all went up to the flat, Mangiarotti pushing the old man roughly ahead of him up the stairs. The old man took off

110 his coat and hat and came to sit at the table where Mangiarotti had placed an open bottle of red wine and three glasses. The old man refused to let go of the briefcase, but held it carefully on his lap. He and Mangiarotti talked for a while in their thick dialect, ignoring me completely. As they talked, the tone of

115 Mangiarotti's voice softened, and I could tell from the way he looked at the wrinkled little man opposite him that, deep down, he was really fond of him. Mangiarotti's problem was that he did not allow himself to show it. My theory was that the old man was a relative of some kind: an uncle, perhaps.

120 It came as something of a shock to me, therefore, when the old man said to me, while Mangiarotti was in the kitchen preparing some pasta for our dinner: 'Do you know, *giovanotto*, I can't stand my son's cooking! He cannot even boil an egg, the idiot, let alone pasta.'

125 'Your son? Signor Mangiarotti's your son?'

The old man shrugged his shoulders as if to say that it was a matter over which he had no control, an unfortunate accident of Nature.

'Now, if you want to taste really good pasta, you should let

me cook for you sometime. I would cook you a dish full of tastes   130
and flavours that you would never forget. What does that idiot
son of mine know about herbs and flavourings? All he knows
is garlic and tomato paste. But, me . . .' At this point, he tapped
the side of his nose again, and nodded towards the briefcase on
his lap. 'Sh!' he whispered. 'Not a word!'   135

I stared at him blankly, and then decided to nod in smiling
agreement. A dim memory from my childhood warned me that
it was not wise to displease an elf. Mangiarotti came in then,
and plonked the food down on the table. It was not bad, but
it wasn't very tasty either. The old man was right: it could have   140
done with more flavour, the flavour that comes from adding just
the right amount and combination of herbs. We finished off the
bottle and started on a second. They say that wine loosens the
tongue, but conversation did not get any easier, and I was quite
relieved when Mangiarotti announced that he was going out to   145
the shop to get some more wine.

As he was leaving, he turned to me, and said, in English so
that his father would not understand: 'Take no notice of that
old fool. His head is full of nonsense. In fact, if I were you, I
wouldn't even bother to talk to him.'   150

It was a cruel thing to say about your own father, I thought.
As soon as he had left the room, the old man turned to me
again.

'So, what do you think, *giovanotto*?' The same unanswerable
question, but this time I was ready for it.   155

'Not bad,' I replied, wondering if it was the answer he wanted.

'Not bad? *Not bad??* What a miserable expression. Pah!
That's the sort of mean little thing that *he* would say,' he said,
nodding towards the door through which Mangiarotti had gone
a minute before. 'No, *giovanotto*, it is not merely "not bad"; it   160
is marvellous. Marvellous. That's the word!' He picked up his
glass and emptied it in a single swallow.

I refilled it for him, and at the same time echoed the word:
'Marvellous. Yes, you're right. It's marvellous.'

165 This seemed to satisfy him. His eyes narrowed and he beckoned to me to lean forward. He began to talk in an urgent whisper, despite the fact that there were only the two of us in the room.

'It's the perfect crime, don't you think?' he said.

170 'Well, yes,' I replied.

'Yes, *giovanotto*, I'm going to be rich! Rich!'

'How exactly . . .?' I began, but he was not to be interrupted.

'Just think! The biggest bank in Paris! And I shall rob it!'

'You mean . . .?' But no question was necessary. Nothing

175 would stop him now from telling me. His eyes shone with excitement.

'Yes, dear boy, I shall simply walk in, fill my briefcase with money and walk out again,' he said. He sat back, his wrinkled elfin face radiating self-confidence. I was certain now that he was

180 completely off his head.

'But, won't somebody try to stop you?' I asked, as gently as I could.

'Ah, that's the beauty of it, my simple young friend. That's the beauty of it: I SHALL BE INVISIBLE!' The last four words came

185 out like a banner headline. He looked anxiously towards the door before continuing. 'Look!' he said. He opened his briefcase, and allowed me to peer in. It was stuffed with what looked to me like dead plants, leaves and blades of grass. 'Herbs, *giovanotto*, herbs. That's the secret. I have perfected a formula to

190 make myself invisible. What do you think of that?'

'Very goo–, er, marvellous!' I replied encouragingly. He was mad, but I hoped that he was harmless. His eyes were fierce with enthusiasm and pride at that moment. He repeated the word 'marvellous' to himself, and then, to my astonishment,

195 slumped back in his chair. Suddenly, his eyes lost their brightness, his face took on an expression of deep misery and his body seemed to shrink even more, like a punctured balloon.

'What's the matter?' I asked gently, thinking he might be ill from too much wine.

I swear I saw tears in his eyes as he replied, in a tiny voice: 200
'I can make *myself* invisible, but I don't know how to make my
briefcase invisible!' It was very difficult for me to keep a straight
face, and I was very glad to hear the sound of Mangiarotti
returning with the wine. As soon as he came into the room, he
sensed the atmosphere. He spoke to me in English, which must   205
have made the old man fear that I might say something about
his secret plans.

'What were you talking about? What has that old fool been
telling you?' Mangiarotti asked suspiciously.

I hate lying, but I did not want to let the old man down, so   210
I just said: 'Herbs. He's been telling me about herbs.'

'What about herbs?'

'About their uses.'

'Hmm,' said Mangiarotti, reassured. 'Well he should know
about herbs. He was once the head chef in one of the best hotels   215
in Rome. The trouble is, he won't accept that he is just a useless
old man now.' Mangiarotti paused to look at his father, who was
sitting very very quietly, as if he were indeed trying to make
himself invisible. Then he added, bitterly: 'You watch! As soon
as my back is turned, the old fool will be off again to that   220
damned ditch collecting herbs. I'm the one who has to go and
fetch him back every time. He's just a bloody nuisance to
himself and to everyone else.'

Mangiarotti went into the kitchen to fetch the corkscrew. The
old man looked across to me, his eyes silently asking me if his   225
secret was still safe. What else could I do? I winked at him and
tapped the side of my nose. The elfin smile that spread across
his face at that moment was a picture.

Gossip

Fred Battersby had a fine collection of married women, and he tried to treat them equally. No favourites. He usually called round on them once a week, staying perhaps for an hour, trying to pay exactly the same amount of attention to each one.

He still remembered the day one of them, Audrey Ball, had 5 stopped him in the street and said: 'I hear you've been to see Ann *twice* this week, and you haven't been to see me once!' Of course she tried to make it sound like a joke, but Fred's sensitive antennae picked up the undertones of jealousy. After that, he was always careful to share himself out, as it were. 10

So it was that Fred had his regular round, calling in turn on Audrey and Ann and Judy and Carol and – but it is unnecessary to list them all: the point is that they were all very fond of Fred, and always very pleased to see him.

'Hello, Fred! Come in! I've just put the kettle on. Would you 15 like a cup of tea?' said one.

'Ah, Fred, I'm so glad to see you. I wonder if you'd give me a hand to move this settee?' said another.

'Good morning, Fred. Sorry if I'm not very cheerful, but I'm worried about my youngest: she's got a terrible cough,' said a 20 third.

'Hello, Fred. How are you? I'm a bit fed up myself. To tell you the truth, Richard and I have had another row,' confided a fourth.

And so it went. Fred was like a counsellor to them. He was 25 a friend, an adviser, a doctor, a priest and a handyman all rolled into one. And Fred loved it. Firstly, he loved it because he was good at it. Fred lived alone, his wife having died a year or two before. He was still no more than middle-aged, a tallish man, not handsome but with a pleasant open face that seemed to encourage people to confide in him. He was good at it because he was one of those rare men who actually *like* women. Of course, most men will tell you, and themselves, that they like women, but the fact is that most men feel more relaxed and comfortable in the company of other men. They *need* women, certainly, as lovers and mothers and housekeepers and admirers, but on the whole they do not actually like them – probably because they do not really understand them.

This is where Fred was different. He enjoyed the company of women, and he understood them. He knew what it was like for married women to look after houses and husbands and children, serving up perhaps twenty meals a week, nursing the family through its problems and illnesses, listening patiently while husbands complained about the boss or the terrible time they had had at work that day. And all the time, these same women were trying to stay attractive and lively. Fred understood all this, and did his best to be a good friend to his married ladies.

'Here you are, Ann. I've brought you some tomatoes from my greenhouse. They'll put the colour back in your cheeks!'

'Audrey, you've had your hair done. It really suits you!'

'Hello, Judy. You're looking a bit tired. Are you sure you're not overdoing things a bit?'

'That's a pretty dress, Carol. What? You made it yourself? I wish I had talent like that.'

He listened to their problems, took an interest in their children, complimented them on their appearance, tried to make them feel important. He even flirted with them sometimes in a light-hearted way that amused them but never offended them. In short, he did all those things that husbands should do, but often forget to do because they are too busy and too wrapped up in themselves.

So, Ann and Audrey and Carol and the rest appreciated Fred when he came round each week to collect the insurance premiums. They looked forward to a friendly chat, a helping hand when they needed one, or simply a break from the boring routine of housework. But Hadley is a small village, and tongues began to wag. The sight of Fred's old bike propped up against Ann Fletcher's front wall or against the side of Carol Turner's house for an hour or more, when everyone knew he only needed to be there two minutes, started the gossip among the older village women.

'I always said he was no good.'

'I think it's a disgrace. She's a married woman with two small children!'

'Her poor husband: he doesn't even suspect what's going on!'

'That Ann Fletcher. Personally, I think she leads him on, you know, actually *encourages* him!'

The worst of these gossips was undoubtedly old Mrs Somersham. Her husband was not only the manager of the local bank, but also chairman of the Parish Council. She told him about her suspicions, but in that indirect way which makes gossip seem more like concern for the welfare of others. Mr Somersham took no notice at first, but then began to wonder. He heard one or two comments from other sources and eventually began to believe the stories about Fred. He thought for a while, and decided to have a quiet word with one of the husbands. As is always the way with these things, it was not long before the other husbands were made aware of the gossip about their wives and the unspeakable Fred Battersby. Well, these men had their pride, so naturally they were sure that their wives were as innocent as angels. But it was clear that these innocent angels were in danger from a widower with a roving eye and the morals of a stray dog. So the husbands of Carol Turner and Ann Fletcher and the rest began to get jealous or angry or sulky, and they began to say unkind things or to drop hints about Fred Battersby in the offhand way that people have when they don't want to look foolish but still want to have their way.

Eventually, the smell of scandal reached too many noses, and
100 something had to happen. Tired of Mrs Somersham's references to the subject, Mr Somersham decided to have another quiet word, this time with his old friend, Porter, who happened to be the managing director of the insurance company that Fred worked for. Just a quiet word was enough. Fred lost his job
105 shortly afterwards. He could feel the cold atmosphere around him and, before long, packed his things and moved to another village several miles away. Mrs Somersham clucked with satisfaction, old Somersham breathed a sigh of relief, the offended husbands relaxed, and peace settled once more over Hadley.

110 For a time, that is. But then, the strangest things began to happen to Fred's married ladies. Not long after Fred's departure, Ann Fletcher had an affair (a real, serious love affair) with an estate agent from Stamford. Then, a month or two later, Audrey Ball just got up one day and walked out on her husband.
115 At about the same time, a rumour started going round that Carol Turner was getting a divorce. And by now, even the local postman was aware that Judy Smith was no longer sleeping in the same bed as her husband. At least, these were the kinds of rumours that reached even Fred Battersby, living in his little
120 caravan in another village some miles away. Not that he took any notice of such stories: Fred's the sort of man who has always refused to listen to gossip.

Crash

It is hard for me now to remember why they brought me here. They have given me a very nice room. It is small: it has a narrow bed, a built-in wardrobe, a table and chair, a wash-basin and a bookcase. The room is small, but it is big enough for me. There is a high window opposite the door. If I stand on tiptoe, 5 I can look out on to green fields. Sometimes, for reasons I do not understand, I don't see fields when I look out, but huge saucer-shaped lights, blinding lights that hurt my eyes. Most of the time I am alone, but sometimes they come and talk to me. I think they come about twice a day, but I am not sure, because 10 I find it difficult to know what time it is, or what day it is, or why I am here.

They always ask me the same questions. Their voices are high-pitched, squeaky. They sound like mice to me. I am used to them now, and I try to be polite. I try very hard to answer 15 their questions. They watch me closely as they interrogate me, their bright, red eyes searching mine to see if I am telling them the truth. But what is the truth? I can remember the awful moments before the crash, the terrible moments when I lost control of the machine. I can remember trying desperately to 20 escape before impact, but I couldn't open the door. I can remember the sensation of spinning and falling and the moment when I hit the ground. I was trapped, crushed by an enormous weight on my chest. I can still hear the sound of my own screams at that moment . . . The rest is blackness. 25

'Who are you?' 'What is your name?' 'Why did you come here?' I have no answers to their questions. They seem to be fascinated by my body. As they talk, they walk round me, reaching up to stroke my arms, to hold my hand, to prod my soft flesh with their sharp fingers. When I am sitting, they like to run their fingers through my tight curly hair, or to touch my face, especially my lips. The first time they touched me, I hated it, but now I am used to it. I don't mind at all, because I know that they mean me no harm. No, that is not true. Sometimes they tie me down on the bed, so that I cannot move at all. I hate that feeling, that feeling of being trapped, unable to escape. Then they come and stick pins into my flesh. I know it sounds silly, but that is what they do. Perhaps they do not mean to hurt me; perhaps they are carrying out tests of some kind, trying to find out more about me and where I come from. I suppose I am as much an alien to them as they are to me.

'Who are you?' they ask in their squeaky voices. I try hard to remember. A name. Any name. If only I could look at myself in a mirror. Perhaps if I saw my face, it would remind me of a name. There is a mirror over the wash-basin, but, when I look into it, I cannot see any reflection. That really frightens me. It is as if I no longer exist. I breathe on the mirror, but it does not mist over. Isn't that how you test for vampires? Am I dead?

'What is your name?' I can think of a dozen names: George, Mary, John, Elizabeth . . . Names of the kings and queens of England. Let's try a name.

'John.'

They stare at me silently, then turn away and chatter together. The one who seems to be in charge comes back and stands in front of me, looking into my eyes accusingly. He points at my chest and shakes his head. He knows that John is a man's name. How can my name be John? Therefore, I deduce, I must be a woman. Female. Interesting. I run my hands over my shiny black skin. Men are hairy. I have no hair on my arms. Therefore I am female. And I am beautiful. Black is beautiful.

Where have I heard that before?' I look down at my arms. Suddenly, they are not black any more – they are white! Hard and cold and white. What have they done to me? And why do my arms suddenly feel so heavy, like lumps of lead. Perhaps they have drugged me. I am afraid again. I want my mummy! A childish frightened cry echoes in my ears. Is it my voice that cries out, childlike, for mother?

'Your name cannot be John,' says the tallest of these squeaking mouse-like creatures. The flashing pink eyes stare at me waiting for an explanation. 'Please tell us the truth.'

'I'm sorry,' I say. 'You're right. My name isn't John. It's . . .' My voice trails away into silence. If only I could see my reflection in the mirror! Then I will know who I am. They leave me to my silence.

After a long time, I get up and go to the mirror. Still no reflection. Nothing. I run my fingers over my face, feeling its bumps and hollows, feeling it as if for the first time, curious. I examine my body, stroking and prodding it the way they do. Again, I explore my face. Whose face is it? How can you recognise your own face? Or your own body? There is a saying: 'I know something like the back of my hand'. I close my eyes and feel the back of my hand. What do I know about this hand? Nothing. I think back to that terrifying moment before the crash. Then I was alive. Then I knew who I was and what I was doing. I was . . . A picture starts to form in the mirror, dimly, like distant trees seen through morning mist. I examine the picture in the mirror as if it were an old faded photograph. I can just make out a table. That's it! There's a table and food, and people eating and talking and laughing . . . I can see a woman, plump and loving, serving the food to the others. The mother of this happy family. My mother? My mother. It is just like a scene from one of those movies about the American Deep South. She looks at me.

'Mary-Jean, stop your day-dreaming, and eat your dinner!' she says.

I run to the door, hammering on it to make them hear.

'Mary-Jean!' I shout. 'My name is Mary-Jean! Listen to me! It's Mary-Jean!'

Nobody comes. I go back to the mirror. It is blank again. That comforting picture of my family has gone. Where is my mother? And where am I, pretty little Mary-Jean, with her tight black curls and her dreamy eyes? The blackness has returned. I try to scream but cannot. Desperately, I throw myself face-down on the bed and cry myself to sleep.

Later, much later. The sound of voices from a long way off. Strong voices, not squeaky mouse-like voices, but firm and businesslike. And bright lights, huge saucers of light, burning through my closed eyelids. Suddenly I am afraid to open my eyes.

'He's coming round, doctor.' It was a woman's voice. I struggled desperately to remember where I was.

'Thank you, nurse.' This was another female voice, the voice of someone who was used to being in charge. It could only be the doctor.

I opened my eyes, not afraid of the lights any more. The doctor was holding my hand and looking down at me. I could see that her eyes were blue behind her pink-framed spectacles.

'Well, young man,' she went on, holding my hand. 'We were very worried about you.'

'Where have I been?' I whispered, realising as I said it that it must have sounded like a very stupid question.

'You've been unconscious for several days, John, my dear. It's been quite a struggle, but you've made it, despite all your broken bones. It looks as if you're going to be all right after all. Just try to get some rest.' She turned to the nurse. 'Mary-Jean, would you give him a sedative, please?' As the nurse approached with the needle full of the sedative fluid, I heard the doctor say to her: 'These youngsters and their fast cars. There ought to be a law against them.'

The nurse made me comfortable, or at least as comfortable as it is possible to be when you are encased from head to toe in plaster. I heard the click-click of her heels on the hard floor as she walked away. It was a comforting sound. Soon I was in a deep, untroubled sleep.

Magic

On the rank at Perth airport, there is often an old London taxi, tall and square and roomy, the sort you can almost stand up in. It looks out of place among the sleek American cars that the other taxi-drivers use. When I arrived there from Britain, I took the taxi and asked the driver how on earth it came to be in Australia. 5

It seems that the taxi was originally imported by a man called Mansell, who had a car-hire business in Perth. He wanted to use it for weddings. He restored it lovingly, lining and carpeting the whole interior with red velvet. Mansell's Red Velvet Taxi was 10 a beauty. It was sure to be a success as a wedding car, as grand as anything that the Queen of England ever rode in.

Sadly, Mansell never used his taxi. On the very day that Mansell finished the car, his wife left him. Nobody knows why. He was broken-hearted, and, as men often do in such cases, he 15 took to drink. One day, he got into his Red Velvet Taxi and drove out towards Allandale, a small settlement on the outskirts of Perth. He ran head on into a eucalyptus tree, and was killed instantly. The taxi was left to rust by the roadside.

'Is that when you got it?' I asked the driver. 20

'Oh no!' he said, sounding almost shocked at the suggestion. 'That was when the old witch, Gooby, took it over.'

'Who?'

'You mean you've never heard of Old Mother Gooby?' he asked in disbelief. 25

'I've only just arrived from England,' I said.

'Well, her real name was Martha Gooby,' he went on. 'But as long as anyone can remember, she was called Old Mother Gooby – though she can't have been more than thirty-five when she came to live in Allandale. She was born old, I reckon. They say she suddenly appeared in Allandale on the very day that Mansell was killed. Anyway, she made her home in the abandoned taxi.'

'What was she like?'

'Squat, like a frog. Stumpy legs. Her face was sort of bright red. Some say it matched the red velvet of the taxi.'

'Did you ever meet her?'

'Me? No, before my time, mate. But people who saw her always talked about her staring eyes. They had a far-away look in them. You know, like sailors' eyes. It comes from spending too much time staring at the horizon.' He was silent for a moment.

'You said she was a witch,' I prompted him. But we had arrived at my hotel, and the conversation came to an end, leaving me unsatisfied.

After finishing my business in Perth, I decided to hire a car and drive out to Allandale. It was a blazing hot day, and the place seemed asleep. I stopped at a small bar in the main street, desperately thirsty. There wasn't another soul in the place, and I had no difficulty in getting into conversation with the barman. His thin face wore the typical barman's bored expression, the expression that says: 'I've seen it all. I know it all. Nothing you can say or do will surprise me.' I told him how surprised I had been to see an old London taxi-cab in the town.

'It's the only one in the whole of Australia,' he said confidently.

'They say some old woman actually lived in it for a while,' I said, hopefully.

He gave a short, humourless laugh. 'So, you've already heard about Old Mother Gooby, have you?'

He confirmed the story about her being a witch. Children,

who know more than grown-ups about the ways of witches, used to frighten each other with stories about her magic powers. They would point at her in the street and call her names – but always from a safe distance. They knew that Old Mother Gooby's magic powers came from the curious stone that she wore in a leather 65 pouch around her neck. She often fingered the pouch, the way a rich lady touches her diamond necklace to reassure herself that it is still there. Nobody had ever seen the stone properly, but the story was that it had aborigine carvings on it. And, as every child knew, the time to beware of Old Mother Gooby was when 70 she stared at you *and* fingered the stone at the same time: that was when she'd turn you into a frog, or something worse, if you didn't immediately cross your fingers and close your eyes.

There were grown-ups, people who should know better, who told similar stories about her. They said that she had put a spell 75 on Mansell, causing his wife to leave him, causing him to take to drink, causing him to crash, causing his death – and all because she wanted his lovely Red Velvet Taxi. People are silly like that. But she did, it has to be admitted, *look like* a witch – especially when she fixed you with her staring far-away eyes, 80 and fingered the pouch with the stone in it.

'But things change,' the barman continued, shrugging his shoulders. 'People forgot the Mansell incident. The kids kept on tormenting her, of course. But, the funny thing was that she began to get a reputation as a "white witch", you know, the sort 85 that use their magic powers to do good. Healing people and that sort of rubbish.'

At that moment, an elderly man came into the bar and ordered a beer. The barman looked at me and put his finger to his lips. I studied the old man discreetly. He was very tall and 90 thin, like a bamboo pole, but he held himself straight. He was quite ugly, for, on top of his bamboo-pole body, he had a small round head with a tiny chin and, to make matters worse, a huge, red nose, like a clown's. He took his beer without a word and went to sit in the corner. 95

'*He* could tell you a thing or two about Old Mother Gooby,' the barman whispered. 'Cockle, his name is, Daniel Cockle. Used to be Police Sergeant Cockle around here before he retired.'

100   Now, if you want to get an Australian old-timer talking, buy him a beer. Some twenty minutes later, I was sitting at Dan Cockle's table, filling his glass and gently coaxing the story out of him.

   'Wonderful woman, she was. Wonderful healing powers. And 105 it all started because of me.' Old Cockle drained his glass, and waited expectantly. He had a fine sense of the dramatic, and an incredible thirst. I refilled his glass, and he continued his story, half talking to himself. I did not interrupt.

   It all started when Sergeant Cockle, as he was in those days, 110 went to see Old Mother Gooby after receiving a complaint that she was lighting dangerous fires to do her cooking on. As he told it, she noticed, as he bent down to enter the taxi, that he held his head very stiffly.

   'Bad back, eh, Sergeant?' she asked. Her voice croaked, like 115 a frog's, for she was not used to talking to people.

   'How did you know?' Sergeant Cockle asked, astonished.

   'Give me your hand,' the old woman said. She took his hand and gazed into his eyes until he began to feel quite uncomfortable. As she stared at him, she took the stone from the leather 120 pouch and began to rub it. The poor man did not know what to expect. Was she going to put a spell on him? Would she start singing out magic nonsense words? He was just about to pull his hand away when she let go.

   'You'll soon be better,' she said.

125   Having first warned about the danger of starting bush fires, he left and forgot the incident.

   There was no sudden miracle cure, but, as the weeks passed by, he noticed that his back pains began to disappear. Being an important man, a police sergeant no less, he could not, of 130 course, admit that it had anything to do with Old Mother Gooby and her magic powers. He did mention it to his wife, though. That was enough. The story of the cure spread quickly. Mrs Cockle herself, without saying anything to her husband, went along one day to the Red Velvet Taxi, hoping that the old woman might be able cure her stomach pains, since the doctors had said they could do nothing. She was scared of the old woman's eyes, scared of her clutching hand, and of the power of the stone with its mysterious carvings. But she went all the same.

'Mrs Gooby, I'm . . .'

'I know who you are. You're Cockle's woman,' the witch said roughly. 'Stomach pains, eh?'

'How did you know about my stomach pains?'

Old Mother Gooby shrugged. 'Give me your hand.'

Again the long, penetrating stare, the rubbing of the stone, and then a sudden dismissal. And again, after several weeks, a wonderful improvement in the painful condition. Mrs Cockle was amazed. Magic or not, it had worked! After that, Old Mother Gooby's reputation spread like wildfire. People whose doctors had given up their cases as hopeless came to see her. People talked about her cures as if they were miracles. As you would expect, there were those who could offer a simple explanation for her success.

'People just believe what they want to believe,' said one.

'If you think you're going to get better, you *will* get better,' said another.

'If you can make yourself *ill* with worry, why can't you make yourself *well* by thinking positive thoughts?' said a third.

One woman, who had read every medical book since Hippocrates and also subscribed to *Reader's Digest*, had no doubt how the old woman performed her miracle cures: 'She uses a technique called "visualisation". She visualises; that is, she makes pictures in her mind of the thing she wants. So, if you go to her with a boil on your nose, she visualises your nose without the boil. Then she just keeps on thinking and thinking and thinking about your nose without the boil on it. Then, one day, hey presto, your boil has gone.'

'What about the aborigine stone? Everyone knows that the aborigines have special powers.'

170 'Well, you can say what you like. I think it's just visualisation.'

And so the stories went. But dozens of people, who had lost faith in their doctors, paid secret visits to the Red Velvet Taxi, and, nine times out of ten, they got better.

175 Old Dan Cockle stopped talking and shook his head. I waited, assuming that this was another of his dramatic pauses. To my astonishment, I saw that silent tears were running down his cheeks.

'Poor old Martha,' he said softly. 'Poor old devil.' It was
180 obvious from the way he spoke and from the look in his eyes that he was talking about a loved one. Romance, it seems, is a magical flower that will blossom in the most unlikely places. I wanted to hear more, but he remained silent, weeping gently to himself. Another beer failed to get him started again.

185 'What happened to her?' I asked at last. He emptied his glass, stood up and put his hat on with the air of a man who has nothing more to say.

'Happened? Nothing happened. Why should anything happen?' He seemed very angry, and left without another word.

190 I turned to the barman. 'Did I say something to upset him?'

'Not your fault, mate. Old Cockle gets like that when he's had a few beers.'

'Do you know what happened to Martha Gooby?'

The barman leant forward. 'Well, the fact of the matter is,
195 after his wife died, old Dan Cockle practically moved in with her. Imagine that! Him and that old toad of a woman! It hardly bears thinking about! Anyway, he bought a caravan and parked it right next to her taxi. Spent all his time there after that.'

'His wife died? When? How? I thought that she was cured.'

200 'Don't ask me! Some people say Old Mother Gooby caused

her death the way she caused Mansell's death – just to get what she wanted.'

'You mean she wanted Dan Cockle?'

'That's how it looks. And he wanted her too. God knows why.'

'You mean they were in love?'

'Love? How should I know? Listen, mate, I'm just telling you what I've heard,' he said sharply. His attitude was clear. The idea of these two ugly people being in love was too much to swallow. Old Dan, tall and bony with his tiny head and his ridiculous nose; she, red-faced and as fat as a toad – no, surely not! Love is the kind of magic that only happens to beautiful people, isn't it?

'What became of Martha Gooby in the end?'

'Well, as I heard it, old Cockle had to go away for a few days. When he got back, he found her lying in her taxi, half dead, hardly able to breathe. A growth in her throat, it was. Anyway, she choked to death before the doctors could do anything.'

'But why hadn't she gone to the doctor earlier, when the growth first started?' I realised at once that it was a silly question. Old Mother Gooby had her own secret cures, whatever they were. Perhaps she had tried to cure herself by visualising her throat without the terrible lump. Perhaps the technique only worked for others.

The rest of the story was simple and sad. Old Dan Cockle sold the caravan and moved back, alone and broken-hearted, into his house in Allandale. Martha's Red Velvet Taxi lay uncared for until an enterprising taxi-driver – the one I had met at the airport – towed it away and restored it. Of course he ripped out all the red velvet. Who wants to ride around in a red-velvet taxi?

I finished my beer and got up to leave. A thought struck me. I turned back to the barman.

'What about the stone?'

'Oh that. It was in her hand when old Cockle found her. Old Cockle's still got it.'

205

210

215

220

225

230

235

33

'Have *you* ever seen it?'

'Yes, he showed it to me once. Just an old stone with some lines scratched on it.'

'Is it aborigine?'

The barman sneered.

'Aborigine, my eye! It's got "Made in Taiwan" written on the back.'

You know how it is: some people just don't want to believe in magic.

A Spray of Heather

[There is nothing peculiar about a person who spends a lot of time sitting in a chair. But what if the chair is a wheelchair? Is there now something peculiar about that person?]

Barcelona is not one of the most beautiful cities in the world: it is a busy, noisy, money-making city. All the same, on a warm spring morning, there are some fine places to spend a quiet hour or two. The Rambles, a tree-lined avenue as broad and as beautiful as any Paris boulevard, is magical at that time of day, a colourful symphony of flowers and sunlight and people.

Andrew Dale was attending an international conference in Barcelona. It was the first time he had been to the city. Like most people, he had heard a lot about the Rambles, and was eager to go there. So he studied the conference programme and convinced himself that he did not want to hear old Professor Thimble's lecture the next morning. (When he was a young man, Thimble developed a theory about a possible relationship between the Basque language and certain Red Indian dialects. He has been giving the same lecture on the subject ever since.)

Andrew had just one tiny problem: he was confined to a wheelchair, the result of an accident on the rugby field when he was at school. What he needed was someone to go with him to the Rambles. That evening, at dinner, he sat next to Tony Willingham, a man he had met once or twice before. It turned out that Tony knew Barcelona very well, and was full of

35

25   enthusiasm for the sights of the Rambles and the nearby Gothic
Quarter. Andrew decided to try his luck. He brought the
conversation round to the subject of Professor Thimble and his
theories.

    'Well, old Thimble's done a lot of work on Basque, I'll
30   admit,' said Tony, 'but, between you and me, I don't think he
has anything new to say.'

    'I think I might give his lecture a miss,' Andrew said casually.

    'You're probably right,' agreed Tony. 'It's a crime to stay in
a stuffy lecture hall when the sun is shining.'

35   'Why don't we sneak off and do some sightseeing?' Andrew
suggested.

    'What a good idea,' Tony said, but his heart sank as he
realised what it would mean to have to take someone round in
a wheelchair. He felt guilty; but, all the same, it wouldn't be
40   much fun for him, pushing a wheelchair around, getting the
damned thing in and out of taxis, lifting it up and down steps,
weaving his way through the narrow crowded streets of the
Gothic Quarter . . . He despised himself for being so selfish, but
couldn't help the way he felt. 'Yes, Andrew,' he went on,
45   putting a brave face on it, 'we'll set off after breakfast. OK?'

    After a while, Tony began to feel better about the idea. Like
a Boy Scout, he would do his good deed for the day. (He didn't
stop to ask himself whether a man who does a good deed
because he *has to do it* is as virtuous as a man who does a good
50   deed because he *wants to do it*. Perhaps it is better to leave such
questions to the philosophers.)

    The two truants set off after breakfast, but first they waited,
like guilty schoolboys, until the other conference delegates had
gone off to Thimble's lecture. Tony wheeled Andrew out into
55   the street and hailed a taxi. To Tony's surprise, it took only a
few seconds to fold the wheelchair and put it in the boot, while
Andrew, using a pair of walking-sticks, eased himself into the
front seat. When they got to the Rambles, the taxi-driver (a rare
man who actually understood about such things) reassembled

the chair, and soon Tony and Andrew were strolling down the centre of the avenue, enjoying the morning sunshine and the colourful displays of the flowersellers. But as the sun got hotter, the cool, narrow side streets which led into the Gothic Quarter looked more and more inviting.

'Is it all right if we go down here?' asked Tony, unsure whether the rough surface of the side street was suitable for Andrew's chair. He was getting used to pushing the chair, and was beginning to feel really good inside, as we all do when we know we are doing a good deed.

'There's no harm in trying,' replied Andrew, whose philosophy ever since his accident had been 'Where there's a will, there's a way'.

Well, despite cobble-stones and kerbs and crowds, they soon got themselves happily lost in the maze of little streets which are characteristic of the old parts of so many cities. They called in at a bar for a cooling drink – fortunately there was only one step – and managed to have a friendly, muddled conversation with the Catalan barman.

'Can you ask him where the toilet is?' Andrew asked Tony. Tony felt a sudden panic. The toilets in these little bars are usually in a tiny basement down a flight of narrow stairs. How on earth was he going to get Andrew to the toilet? At that moment, he wished he were sitting safely in old Thimble's boring lecture instead of . . . Tony pushed the unworthy thought from his mind. He asked the barman. As he feared, the toilet was down a flight of steep stairs. The barman looked at Andrew, or rather at the wheelchair, for it often happens that the occupant of the wheelchair becomes invisible at such times.

'No problem!' he said cheerfully, instructing Tony to lift the bottom of the wheelchair while he lifted the top. Andrew tried to explain to Tony that there was a much simpler solution, namely that he could easily get out of the chair and go down the stairs on his sticks. It was a waste of time protesting. The well-meaning barman had taken charge of the situation. He and

95   Tony bundled Andrew and the chair down the stairs as if they
were handling a sack of coal. Andrew sighed inwardly and
allowed himself to be banged and buffeted into the toilet.

Tony was glad when they left the bar, because he had become
aware of Andrew's impatience at the way the barman had taken
100 over. After all, who knew better the problems of getting around
in a wheelchair than Andrew himself? They wandered on in
silence until they came to the cathedral.

'Let's have a look inside, shall we?' suggested Andrew.

Now, the medieval architects and builders of our cathedrals
105 were wonderful fellows, but they did not allow for people in
wheelchairs. Tony's heart sank when he saw the high steps and
the stone stairways which take you down into the cathedral, but
Andrew didn't seem to notice them. There was a man in a
uniform on duty at the main entrance, and he lent a hand to get
110 Andrew and the chair down the stairs. As they went around,
Tony found that he could not concentrate on the majestic Gothic
interior of the huge building. He was unable to forget the
moment in the bar when he had wished to be somewhere else,
a long way away from wheelchairs. What a terrible thing to
115 think! How could he be so uncaring, so self-centred?

He was glad to get out of the cathedral. It was too big: it was
overpowering, even gloomy and depressing in the end. Tony
pushed Andrew slowly down a pretty street by the side of the
cathedral where the street-musicians play. As they emerged from
120 the street, a gypsy woman came up to them and offered Tony
a spray of heather, a sweet-scented herb that is supposed to
bring good luck. Tony was so startled that he did not react. The
woman then leant over the wheelchair and pinned the spray of
heather to Andrew's lapel. Andrew smiled at her, wishing he
125 had the words to say thank you. The woman smiled back at
him, then turned to Tony, begging, in that whining way that
gypsies have, for a little money in return for the gift of heather.

Tony felt in his pocket and found that he had no change. He
certainly didn't want to give her a five-hundred-peseta note. He

bent down and whispered to Andrew: 'You haven't got any   130
change, have you, Andrew? We'd better give her a few pesetas
or we'll never get rid of her.'

Andrew started to root in his jacket pocket, but, before he
could take out any coins, the gypsy woman, realising what he
was doing, exploded in anger. She turned on Tony and started   135
screaming at him, cursing him and calling him terrible names.
She had a thick Andalusian accent and her voice was so distorted
with anger and hatred that he couldn't understand her words.
Her meaning was clear, though: how *could* he ask this poor crippled man in the wheelchair to pay for the heather? How *could*   140
he take money from this poor suffering child of God? It was an
awful moment for Tony: there was no chance of explaining the
truth to her. Finally, having used up every swear-word and
every curse in her vigorous Andalusian dialect, she turned to
walk away. But just as she was leaving, she reached across,   145
snatched the spray of heather from Andrew's lapel and put it
back in her basket. Andrew laughed. He found the whole incident very, very funny. Tony, on the other hand, didn't say
a word all the way back to the hotel.

The Wrong Pig

Bruno Kaufmann and I were as different as chalk and cheese, but we were friends. He was a handsome young man, well-built and athletic. He was good at all kinds of sports, an excellent driver, a great dancer – in short, he was one of those people who seem to do everything well. He came from a wealthy German family and had plenty of money. It is true that he liked to show off, but he was very easygoing and generous, so he was also very popular – especially with the girls.

We met in Florence, where we were both studying Italian. Bruno's father owned a business in Rome, and had sent Bruno to learn Italian before taking over the Rome office. Bruno attacked the language with great enthusiasm. Unlike me, he didn't care how many mistakes he made, as long as he could make himself understood. As a result, he was soon fluent. He was the one who did all the talking, especially when it came to chatting up the girls.

As I say, Bruno and I got on well together, despite our different characters, partly because I had one quality which he liked: I was a very good listener. Since he kept on falling in love, he always needed someone to listen while he described how the latest girl in his life had stolen his heart, or how the last one had broken it.

All this changed the day we met Eveline and Suzanne Louvier. Eveline and Suzanne were identical twins, or at least that is what they told us. Eveline was older by only twenty minutes, but she was every inch the older sister. Although they were the same height, Eveline seemed taller than her rather plump sister, Suzanne. Perhaps it was the way Eveline held herself, for she always walked very upright, like a queen.

30 Anyway, Bruno couldn't take his eyes off these two Swiss beauties from the first day they appeared at the school, and he quickly made their acquaintance. Poor Bruno! Like a child faced with a choice between two flavours of ice-cream, he couldn't make up his mind which one he wanted. First he ran after

35 Eveline, who seemed to be amused by him, for she teased him endlessly. Then, for a while, he turned his charm on Suzanne, who fell for his generous nature and his dark good looks. Then he ran back to Eveline again. We went out in a foursome several times before it became clear that Eveline's game of playing hard

40 to get had paid off. For perhaps the first time in his life, Bruno was the one who had to do the chasing. The result was clear to see: he was soon head over heels in love with her. And it really was different this time. When he talked about her, his eyes were misty. He became restless when they were apart, not eating,

45 unable to study – in other words, he showed all the symptoms of the illness we call 'love'.

 As for Suzanne, he had a simple solution: 'Chris, you like Suzanne, don't you?'

 The fact was that I didn't know what I felt about Suzanne.

50 I became tongue-tied when I was with her. She was so much more beautiful and intelligent than any girl I had ever met. 'She's very nice, Bruno,' I said.

 'You know, Chris,' he replied, 'you are the most unromantic person I know! She's not just "very nice" – she's a wonderful

55 girl. And you know she likes you very much, don't you?'

 'Does she?'

 'Of course! That's settled, then!'

 Bruno had decided that I should look after the younger sister, leaving him free to concentrate on the older one. I didn't mind

60 at all, for I really liked being with Suzanne, despite my shyness.

Although I would never have said so to Bruno, I thought she was a much warmer person than Eveline, who always reminded me of the Ice Queen. Never mind, the important thing was that Bruno and Eveline seemed well suited. Like him, she was an outdoor type, and good at everything she did. 65

There was only one problem: Suzanne was also in love with Bruno. Suzanne hid her feelings very well from the others, but I could see at once what she was going through. I saw the way she looked at Bruno, and the way she trembled when he, in his easygoing way, would take her in his strong arms and give her 70 a hug, or kiss her playfully, the way you hug and kiss younger sisters. Her pain was real and terrible, and I did my best to comfort her, because I hated to see her so unhappy.

One day, Bruno came to see me, his expression serious. 'Chris, can I talk to you?' Before I could reply he went on: 75 'What do you think of Eveline? Isn't she fantastic?' He kept on asking me such questions, as if he needed to reassure himself that he wasn't dreaming, and that this wonderful girl really did exist. Finally he came to the point.

'The fact is, Chris, that I'm thinking of asking her to marry me.' 80
I hid my astonishment. 'Have you said anything to her?'
'Not yet. But I'm serious, Chris. Look, you're my best friend. What do you think?'
'It does seem a bit . . . sudden, Bruno. After all, you've only known each other a few weeks.' 85

He nodded at me, but he wasn't really listening. He had already made his mind up. He telephoned his father that evening, and I knew enough German to understand that he was discussing Eveline. At one point, Bruno said 'That's right, *Vati*,' (how odd to hear him call his father 'Daddy' – suddenly, Bruno 90 was a little boy again) 'Louvier, the Swiss manufacturer.'

I have no idea what his father thought about his son's plans, but Bruno seemed very happy as he put the phone down. 'Come on, Chris,' he called cheerfully. 'Let's go and meet the girls. Why don't we go to the Cucina for a celebration dinner?' 95

43

The Cucina Casalinga was one of our favourite restaurants. It was a small family restaurant, cheap and cheerful, and always full of interesting characters. I guessed that he had chosen it that night because he always felt at home there – on first name terms with the owner and his wife, and popular with the regular customers. Perhaps he needed to be on home ground if this was to be the night for 'popping the question'. As it turned out, he could not have made a worse choice.

We met the girls and walked together along the Arno, enjoying the cool evening air. It was March – a good time to be in Florence, with the promise of spring in the air, but before the start of the tourist season. Eveline and Bruno were ahead of us, as usual, leading the way. They were arm in arm and talking softly, as lovers do.

Suzanne carefully looked away, staring instead across the Arno. She slipped her hand in mine and murmured softly: 'Isn't Florence wonderful, Chris! Wouldn't you like to stay here for ever?'

The feeling of her hand in mine, the scent of her perfume and the magical Florentine setting was almost more than I could bear. At that moment I felt both happier and more miserable than I had been in my whole life.

We arrived at the Cucina thirsty and hungry. It was crowded as usual, filled with the noise of lively conversation and the smell of good cooking. The owner greeted us like long lost friends, paid compliments to the girls and sat us at the one table I would have preferred to avoid: the one next to Clara and Marietta. Now, Clara and Marietta, despite their names, were two men in their late twenties. For some reason, they were usually dressed and made up as women whenever we saw them. They were regulars at the Cucina and no one took any notice of them; they were part of the scene. Although my mother always used to say 'It takes all sorts to make a world', I have to say frankly that Clara and Marietta made me feel uncomfortable.

But for Bruno, they were just a couple of odd characters. He winked at me, as if to say 'Let's have some fun', and then turned to greet them cheerfully: '*Buona sera, signorine!* Good evening, ladies! How are you this lovely evening?'

They returned his greeting, believing him to be a good-natured fellow, not one to make fun of them. Then, to my horror, he introduced them to Eveline and Suzanne. The girls smiled weakly, trying hard not to stare, trying to be sophisticated. Suzanne, in her simple open-hearted way, tried not to notice that the two *signorine* were in fact men, but Eveline's expression was cold and unfriendly. She managed an insincere '*Buona sera*' and turned her head away. Bruno pretended not to see Eveline's reaction. He winked at me again and continued his conversation with Clara and Marietta.

Finally, he turned back to us, rubbing his hands and exclaiming: 'Well, now, I don't know about you three, but I'm starving. What shall we have to eat?'

I was glad that Clara and Marietta left shortly afterwards, but I'm afraid the damage had been done.

As soon as they had gone, Suzanne leaned across to me: 'They *were* men, weren't they, Chris?'

'Yes, Suzanne.'

'Well, why were they wearing women's clothes? Are they going to a fancy-dress party?'

'I don't think so, Suzanne,' I replied, conscious of Eveline's face, white with anger. Please, Suzanne, I prayed silently, please change the subject!

'Do you know them?'

'Not really. We've seen them a couple of times before.'

'But why do they dress like that? I mean, are they actors? Or are they students, perhaps, doing it for a bet?'

Bruno burst in: 'You mean Clara and Marietta?' He grinned. 'Who knows? And who cares? They're really quite stupid, don't you think?' Although he was smiling as he spoke, his words sounded cruel and unfeeling.

Suzanne was not so much shocked by the odd couple as

135

140

145

150

155

160

165

curious: she simply wanted to know more about them. Not so
Eveline. She was very angry. First, Bruno had introduced her
to two people that she would never have dreamt of speaking to.
Then he had turned his back on her and gone on talking to
170 them. He even *liked* them!

Bruno could see that Eveline was very quiet, but he still
seemed unaware that she was also very upset. 'What's wrong,
darling? Aren't you feeling well?' he asked, putting on his most
innocent voice.

175 'You know perfectly well what's wrong! How *could* you introduce us to those awful creatures? I've never felt so humiliated
in all my life!'

'Who? Clara and Marietta? Oh, come on, Eveline, don't be
so stuffy! I was just having a bit of fun.'

180 'Please stop using those stupid names!' Things were going
from bad to worse. What had started out as a wonderful evening
was turning completely sour. Eveline hardly said another word.
She picked at her food for a time before saying in an icy voice:
'Bruno, please take me home.'

185 I prefer to forget the rest of that evening: Eveline stonily
silent; Bruno sulking, irritated with Eveline because she
couldn't take a joke; and Suzanne near to tears, hating Eveline's
anger and Bruno's black mood.

Well, as you can guess, this was the beginning of the end.
190 After the incident at the Cucina, Bruno and Eveline had several
rows. As often happens, they said cruel things to each other in
anger which they could not take back afterwards. She accused
him of being childish; he accused her of being a snob; and so
it went on. I kept out of the way, because I cannot stand rows.
195 When they finally broke up, Bruno was very upset, like a child
with a broken toy. He came round to see me about a week later,
and poured his heart out. I just listened. There was nothing I
could say. I suppose I felt sorry for him, even though he had
brought it on himself. He then told me how, since Eveline had
200 finished with him, he had spent a lot of time with Suzanne.

'Suzanne has been so good to me, Chris,' he said. 'I had never realised how wonderful she is. You know, she is a really warm, generous person. To tell you the truth, Eveline can be very unfeeling. And she has no sense of humour.'

He was silent for a while, lost in his thoughts. I thought of poor, sweet Suzanne. What a difficult situation it must be for her: on the one hand, wanting to let him know that she loved him; on the other, unable to go against her sister. His voice suddenly broke in on my thoughts.

'You know, Chris,' he said, 'I really think that I made the wrong choice from the start. As we say in German, "*Ich habe das falsche Schwein geschlachtet*" – I killed the wrong pig!'

The words went through me like a knife, especially the ugly word *geschlachtet*, killed. It was like the English word 'slaughter', which means to kill an animal for its meat. The image was horrible. And how could he use the word *Schwein*, pig, to talk about Eveline or Suzanne? My sweet Suzanne. At that moment I realised that I did not like Bruno Kaufmann after all.

205

210

215

Wild Mushrooms

October is the month when Catalans go mad. And it is all because of ugly-looking pieces of vegetable matter which they call *bolets* or wild mushrooms. The English are suspicious of wild mushrooms. They eat only one kind, an amazing species which grows on supermarket shelves already hygienically wrapped. An Englishman's mushrooms are white and tasteless. They are safe, but they are boring. As far as the English are concerned, any mushroom which grows wild is dangerous and best avoided. But, for Catalans, the great hunt for wild mushrooms in October is like a religious crusade. They know that there are many varieties of *bolets* which are delicious to eat. This is why, in October, every self-respecting Catalan becomes a *boleteire* and goes off into the countryside to the spot where his favourite species grows. Mr Mushroom goes off quietly, though, to the secret places which only he knows about – or so he believes.

Meanwhile, patient Catalan housewives sit in their kitchens, dreading the moment when their husbands will return with baskets full of wild mushrooms which have to be sorted and washed and cooked. Of course there will be too many, and Mrs Mushroom will throw a lot of them away unused. But she will not tell her husband, because she knows how proud he is of his afternoon's work. It is a harmless sort of madness, and an old tradition with these proud, hard-working people. Some say that the Catalans do not really enjoy eating their wild mushrooms:

49

the taste they enjoy comes from knowing that the *bolets* did not cost anything! The tradition is so strong that even people who work and live in the big cities like Barcelona, and who have lost all contact with the countryside, will be struck with the madness
30 and rush out on a fine Sunday morning in October. Clever restaurant owners offer dishes made from various species of wild mushrooms as a Sunday lunch-time speciality, so that these townies can say they have eaten them even if they couldn't find their own in the woods. ·

35 So, on an October Sunday morning, Cristofol Balaguer, normally a quiet, hard-working businessman, announced to his family that he had decided to take them to the country for lunch. His wife, Nuria, sighed, for she recognised at once the signs of the *boleteire*'s madness. The children said nothing,
40 because they knew that it was useless to argue against a thousand years of Catalan tradition.

'That will be very nice, darling,' Nuria said, trying to put a brave face on it.

'I thought we could go to Can Lluis,' Cristofol said. It was
45 not a suggestion, but a command. Can Lluis was a typical *bolet* restaurant. It was also close to a wooded hillside where, according to Cristofol, some excellent varieties grew in a secret spot known only (he believed) to the Balaguer family.

'Oh dear,' Nuria sighed to herself. 'Here we go again!'
50 'What a good idea!' she said brightly.

Just before they left the house, Nuria waited until Cristofol was out of the room, and then made a hurried phone-call. Moments later, the family Balaguer were in the car heading out of Barcelona. They passed Montserrat and then took a right-
55 hand turn to go to . . . But no, it would not be fair to tell you the place, or you might go there one day and find the place where the Balaguer *bolets* grow.

Cristofol was humming and whistling to himself. The hunter's instinct made his eyes shine and his heart beat faster. Nuria
60 wore the sort of expression that you can see on the pictures of

saints in Spanish churches, a mixture of silent suffering and
endless patience. The children were playing a sort of I-Spy
game, in which it was easy, and therefore very tempting, to
cheat. It was not long before they were screaming angrily at each
other. In other words, the Balaguer family was like a thousand   65
others on a Sunday morning. But nothing could stop the feeling
of joy in Cristofol's breast as they approached their destination.

They arrived rather early at Can Lluis, so the restaurant was
only half full. The family sat at a table near the window which
looked out on to the wooded hillside at the back. With typical   70
Catalan hospitality their old friend Jordi Puig, who owned the
restaurant, came out to greet them. After the usual greetings
– 'Is it already a year since you were last here?' – and the
compliments – 'You look more beautiful every time I see you,
Senyora', and 'You are a very lucky man, *Senyor* Balaguer!' –   75
he signalled to the waiter to bring some olives and drinks for
everyone. Then, the moment came, the moment which Nuria
dreaded.

'I'm just going for a little walk, darling. I won't be long,'
Cristofol said. His impatience to be off was painfully obvious.   80

'Can we come too, daddy?' the children asked.

'No,' said their mother. 'Daddy wants to go on his own.' How
well she understood the mind of the *boleteire*!

After a while, she and the children grew tired of waiting, so
Nuria decided to order something to eat. They were about half   85
way through their soup when Cristofol came back into the
restaurant. Actually, he did not simply 'come back' into the
restaurant: he 'made an entrance', as an emperor might appear
before his subjects. All heads turned to watch him. His trousers
were covered with red dust and his hair was untidy, but nobody   90
noticed this. All eyes were on the bundle which he was holding
above his head. It was his red spotted handkerchief, and it was
stuffed full with something.

'*Rovellons!*' he said triumphantly to everyone in the room.
'I have just picked them from the secret place which my grand-   95

father told me about!' Now, *rovellons* are the most prized species of all. They are orange in colour and covered with green specks: just the sort of wild mushroom that would cause an Englishman to turn green himself. But Catalans know better: the *rovellon*, despite its appearance, is delicious.

There was a great cheer from the company. Here was a real man! Here was the true *boleteire*! Cristofol's eyes were bright with his great achievement. He looked for, and got, the smile of congratulation from his wife, and an enthusiastic clapping of hands from the children. The restaurant owner came over to the table and added his congratulations.

'We shall have them for lunch, Jordi, if you will be kind enough to cook them for us. You know how we like them: plenty of garlic,' Cristofol said.

'Of course, *Senyor* Balaguer. It will be our pleasure. Nothing tastes so good as the wild mushrooms which one has picked oneself, don't you agree?'

And, to tell the truth, the meal of *rovellons* which the Balaguer family ate that day at Can Lluis was magnificent, a feast, something to make you feel more Catalan, something to remember during those terrible months in the year when there are no wild mushrooms in the woods. Even the children, who secretly preferred beefburgers, left clean plates, and agreed once again that Father's *rovellons* were the best they had ever tasted.

The restaurant owner, Jordi Puig, came to their table once more after they had finished their meal. Now it was his turn to receive the compliments.

'The *rovellons* were excellent, Jordi,' confirmed Cristofol. 'Excellently cooked. Just the right amount of garlic to bring out their flavour. My congratulations!'

Jordi Puig made the sort of noise you make when you wish to show modesty in the face of a compliment, a sort of oshkosh-koshkosh sound. As he turned away, his eyes met Nuria's, and a message flashed between them. Anyone who had seen that secret look might have thought that they were lovers. What they

knew – and what father and the children did not know – was
that the wild mushrooms that Cristofol had picked on the hillside were not in their stomachs but in the dustbin. Cristofol
could never recognise *rovellons*, but always managed to pick a
similar orange-coloured species which was highly poisonous. Mr   135
Puig, a man of great tact and diplomacy, said nothing. He
simply substituted some fresh *rovellons* which he had managed
to get that morning, following an urgent phone-call from a
patient and long-suffering *Senyora*. It was not the first time he
had received such a call, and, as he looked into *Senyora*   140
Balaguer's eyes, he knew it would not be the last: there is an
October in Catalunya every year.

Summer-blue Eyes

Oh God, I'm so fat! I used to have a nice firm bosom and slim hips. Look at me now. Flat on top and fat round the middle. Forty-seven, fat and fading fast. Skin's not too bad, though. Not too good either. This is a terrible mirror! It shows up all the lines on my face. Lines give a woman's face character. Those aren't lines: they're wrinkles. Let's call a spade a spade. Hmm. Oh, come on, pull yourself together. Stop feeling sorry for yourself.

What was that? Sfax? Did the newsreader say Sfax? Damn this radio! It needs a new battery. Yes, it's a programme about Tunisia, so he must have said Sfax. Fancy hearing it again after all these years! Sfax. No, not 'Sfacks'. 'Sfa*kh*', like the 'ch' in 'loch', I think. I never did learn to pronounce it properly.

'Hello. I am Tunisian. I am from Sfax.' His first words to me, uninvited, unexpected.

Fancy remembering the exact words of a conversation I had twenty years ago! (Twenty? No, nearer thirty. Where did all the years go?) I met him on the coach from London to Oxford. I remember, we were the last ones in the queue at Victoria Coach Station, and there was only one seat left. He got on first, and I sat next to him.

'Are you going to Oxford?' he asked.

What a silly question! I was on the Oxford coach, wasn't I? Oh dear, I thought. He's trying to pick me up. Why do men always think that a woman on her own is fair game, just waiting

55

for a man to come along and turn his oily charm on them? Men. Anyway, as it turned out, he wasn't trying to pick me up. He was just being friendly. He was very sweet, really. He was sort of innocent. Childlike. I found that very hard to resist.

30 'Do you live in Oxford?'

'Yes,' I told him. 'I'm a student.'

When you said that, everyone thought you were at the University. Actually, I was a student nurse at the Radcliffe Hospital, but it sounded better if you just said you were a
35 student.

'Please tell me your name.' No, he wasn't just another tiresome male trying it on. He was just being friendly.

'Sylvia.'

'Silvie.'

40 'No, not Silvie. Sylvi*a*.'

'Silvi*aaa*.'

The way he drew out the last vowel was really beautiful. A shiver ran down my spine. When he said my name it was like a caress, like the caress of his hand on my cheek, like the way
45 he ran his fingers through my hair, later.

How is it possible to meet someone at nine-thirty in the morning and be head over heels in love with them by midday? That's what happened to us. He was very good-looking. No, he was beautiful. His eyes were so blue, the colour of summer
50 skies. And his hair was fair, almost red. I loved the feel of his tight curls under my fingers. Blue eyes. Blue loving eyes. Funny, an Arab with fair hair and blue eyes.

He was on holiday, I remember, and had just one day to see Oxford before going back to Tunisia. To Sfax.

55 I was young and green and pretty then. I wish I still felt as young and pretty now. We spent the whole of that day together. It was glorious weather. June's the best month to be in England. I can still feel the warm sun on my neck as we walked through the gardens of St John's College. I can still feel the warmth of
60 his lips the first time he kissed me, the warmth of his body

against me. I remember being terrified that I might start to
sweat. Everyone was terrified of BO – 'body odour' – in those
days. I can remember how cool and dry *his* hands were when
he caressed me . . .

Is it really possible to remember such things? Come on, you're   65
a respectable, middle-aged, married woman. Get on with the
housework and forget all this nonsense.

It's amazing. I can remember the smells and the sounds of
that wonderful June day. I can remember the dizzy feeling of
falling in love. Hands, hands holding, touching, caressing. And   70
the sweet words, and the sweet moments of silence when only
our eyes talked. We made love, I remember, on the bank of the
River Cherwell. Made love. Nowadays people 'have sex' – what
an ugly expression! No, we made love, we *created* love with our
eyes and our sighs and our kisses. It was all very innocent. And   75
so, so beautiful.

Come on, Silvia – 'Silviaaaa' – you cannot afford to cry. You
look dreadful enough as it is, without getting your eyes all red
and puffy. Robert will be home soon. He's a good husband. I'm
very lucky.   80

After he left – I saw him on to the coach back to London –
I went back to the Nurses' Hostel, locked myself in my room
and cried my eyes out. I had the most terrible migraine. I was
ill, really ill, for three whole days. Love. Happiness or pain?
Both. I suppose I knew, even then, that I would never see you   85
again, my fair-skinned Arab. But I saw you a thousand, a
million times in my dreams. Even now I can see your clear blue
eyes, hear your soft, warm voice, feel your hand stroking my
hair. I can still remember too the way we held on to each other,
fighting back the feeling of sadness creeping up on us as the   90
evening and the moment of parting got nearer and nearer . . .

When was it I met Robert? It must have been about two years
after I left the Radcliffe, three years after you took the coach
and went out of my life forever. Now with Robert and me, it
was no whirlwind romance! It took us ages to make up our   95

57

minds to get married. Ages after we met, I finally told Robert
to marry me. Well, there was no point in waiting for *him* to
make the decision. Poor Robert! I do love you, Robert, even if
you are just a little bit boring sometimes, even if you are getting
a bit fat round the middle. Like me. Ah well. What it was to
be young and pretty and green and slim! Sfax. I never thought
I'd hear that word again. Yes, he was handsome, my lover for
a day, my sweet Tunisian. Ah, my long lost lover, with your
summer-blue eyes and your springtime smile, how I loved you!
Now, nearly thirty years on, sweet man, I cannot, for the life
of me, remember your name.

The Joker

It was a very happy funeral, a great success. Even the sun shone
that day for the late Henry Ground. Lying in his coffin, he was
probably enjoying himself too. Once more, and for the last time
on this earth, he was the centre of attention. Yes, it was a very
jolly affair. People laughed and told each other jokes. Relatives   5
who had not spoken for years smiled at each other and promised
to stay in touch. And, of course, everyone had a favourite story
to tell about Henry.

'Do you remember the time he dressed up as a gypsy and
went from door to door telling people's fortunes? He actually   10
made £6 in an afternoon!'

'I was once having dinner with him in a posh restaurant.
When the wine-waiter brought the wine, he poured a drop into
Henry's glass and waited with a superior expression on his face,
as if to say "Taste it, you peasant. It's clear that you know   15
nothing about wine." So Henry, instead of tasting it, the way any
normal person would do, dipped his thumb and forefinger into
the wine. Then he put his hand to his ear and rolled his forefinger and thumb together as if he were *listening* to the quality
of the wine! Then he nodded to the wine-waiter solemnly, as   20
if to say "Yes, that's fine. You may serve it." You should have
seen the wine-waiter's face! And how Henry managed to keep
a straight face, I'll never know!'

'Did you hear about the practical joke he played when he was
a student, the one with the road-menders. Some workmen were   25

59

digging a hole in the road. First, Henry phoned the police and told them that some *students* were digging a hole in the road, and that he didn't think it was a very funny thing to do. Then he went to the workmen, and told them that some students had dressed up as policemen and were coming to tell them to stop digging the hole! Well, you can imagine what happened! Total confusion!'

'Yes, old Henry loved to pull people's legs. Once, when he was invited to an exhibition of some abstract modern painter's latest work, he managed somehow to get in the day before and turn all the paintings upside down. The exhibition ran for four days before anyone noticed!'

'His father, poor man, could never understand why Henry did such crazy things.'

'It's hard to believe that Henry was a Ground when you think how different he was from his brothers.'

Yes, it was difficult to believe that he was a Ground. He was born into an unimportant but well-to-do Midlands family. He was the youngest of five sons. The Grounds were a handsome lot: blue-eyed, fair-haired, clever and ambitious. The four older boys all made a success of their lives. They married beautiful, buxom girls of good family, and produced children as fair and handsome and clever as themselves. The eldest became a clergyman; the second ended up as the headmaster of a famous public school; the third went into business and became disgustingly rich; the fourth followed in his father's footsteps and became a solicitor. Which is why everybody was amazed when the youngest Ground, Henry, turned out to be a lazy good-for-nothing.

Unlike his brothers, he had brown eyes and dark hair, but he was every bit as handsome and charming, which made him quite a ladykiller. And, although he never married, there is no doubt at all that Henry Ground loved women. He also loved eating, drinking, laughing, talking and a thousand other activities which don't make money or improve the human condition.

One of his favourite pastimes was doing nothing. His idea of an energetic afternoon when the sun was shining was to sit under a shady tree, with a pretty companion by his side, and all the time in the world to talk of this and that, to count the blades of grass, and to learn the songs of the bees that buzzed around 65
him.

What a worthless fellow! Some people whispered that his real father was not the respectable Mr Ground at all, but a wild gypsy who had come one day to the house and had swept Mrs Ground off her feet with his dancing black eyes and his wicked 70
country ways. It was a good story, juicy and romantic, but surely untrue. One thing *was* sure: you couldn't help liking Henry Ground and his talent for making you laugh. Henry Ground was, above all else, a joker.

Anyway, the stories went on even while the coffin was being 75
lowered into the grave. People held handkerchiefs to their eyes, but their tears were tears of laughter, not sadness. Afterwards, there was a funeral breakfast, by invitation only. It was attended by twelve of Henry's closest friends. Henry Ground had asked his brother, Colin, to read out his will during the funeral break- 80
fast. Everyone was curious about Henry Ground's will. Henry had been in debt all his life, hadn't he? What could he possibly have to leave in a will?

Colin cleared his throat. 'Ahem! If you are ready, ladies and gentlemen.' Everyone settled down expectantly. Colin opened 85
the will, and began to read it out in a singsong voice.

'I, Henry Ground, being of sound mind . . . last will and testament . . . do hereby bequeath . . . '

The legal phrases rolled on and on, and the audience grew impatient to get to the important part. It came soon enough. 90
When Colin announced that Henry Ground, despite his repu-tation as a good-for-nothing, had invested his money very wisely, and was in fact worth at least three-quarters of a million, everyone gasped. But who was going to get it? Eyes narrowed and throats went dry. 95

'You are all such dear friends of mine,' Colin went on, reading out Henry Ground's words in a monotone, which, in other circumstances, would have sent everyone to sleep, 'that I cannot decide which of you to leave my money to.' Colin paused. In the silence, you could have heard a pin drop. He resumed. 'So, dear friends, I have set you a little competition. Each of you in turn must tell the funniest joke he or she can think of, and the one who gets the most laughter will inherit my fortune. Colin will be the sole judge of the best joke.'

'So, ladies and gentlemen,' said Colin, putting the will down on the table, 'it's up to you now. Who will go first? May I suggest that you go in alphabetical order of surnames?'

The first person stood up and told a very funny joke about an Englishman who fell in love with his umbrella. When he finished, he was in tears of laughter, for he always laughed at his own jokes. The rest of the company remained *absolutely silent*. You could tell from their red faces and their screwed-up eyes that they found the joke funny, but not one of them was prepared to laugh, and give him the chance to win the competition. The second told a story about a three-legged pig, which was so good that, some years later, MGM made a cartoon of it. When she sat down, the others buried their faces in their handkerchiefs, coughed, pretended to sneeze, dropped pencils under the table – anything to cover up their laughter. And so it went on, joke after wonderful joke, the sort of jokes that make your sides ache. And nobody dared to laugh!

You know what it's like when you want to laugh, but cannot. It happens in classrooms all the time. Somebody starts to giggle, and then tries to stop. Immediately three or four others will want to giggle. The desire to laugh spreads like an infection, and soon the entire class is choking, while the teacher looks round baffled, wondering what all the snuffling noises are.

Well, by the time the last joke had been told, every one of the twelve was sitting perfectly still, desperately holding in the laughter which was bursting to get out. Their suppressed laughter had built up such a pressure: it was like a volcano ready to erupt.

Silence. Painful silence.

Suddenly, Colin sneezed. A perfectly ordinary sneeze. Atishoo. Then he took out a ridiculously large spotted-red handkerchief and blew his nose. Bbbrrrrrrppp.

That was enough. Someone burst out laughing, unable to hold it in any longer. That started the others off. In no time, everyone was doubled up, tears streaming from their eyes, their shoulders heaving as wave after wave of laughter erupted like lava from a volcano. Of course, they were not just laughing at the sneeze, nor even at the twelve jokes. No, they were laughing at themselves as it dawned on them that Henry Ground had led them into his last, and funniest, practical joke, setting their need to laugh against their greed for money.

When, at long last, the laughter died down, Colin cleared his throat once more. 'Forgive my little piece of theatre,' he said, his eyes twinkling. 'I have been practising that sneeze for a week or more.' He folded the enormous handkerchief and stuffed it into his pocket. 'Henry's idea, of course,' he added, unnecessarily: all twelve guests realised they had been been set up beautifully.

'Ahem! May I read you the rest of the will now?' Colin asked.

'My friends,' the last paragraph began, 'forgive me, but I couldn't resist playing one last little joke on you. It's good to know that your love of laughter finally overcame your love of money.'

Colin paused, letting the meaning of the words sink in. Then he read out the final part of the late Henry Ground's last will and testament.

'My friends, thank you for letting me have the last laugh. As for the money: because I love you all, my fortune will be divided equally among you. Enjoy your share, and think of me whenever you hear laughter.'

The company fell silent. For the first time that day, there was a feeling of sadness in the air.

If There is Water

With her thin face and her bony body poking through her light cotton dress, Domingues looked about fifteen. In fact she was, as far as she knew, at least twenty-eight years old. Her smooth black skin was surprisingly shiny, as if she had rubbed oil on it. Marina, on the other hand, was quite light-skinned, a *mestiça*, of mixed African and European parentage. The two girls – it was difficult to think of them as women – waited patiently outside Zé Ribeiro's office. Zé was the resident Project Director in Lubango, the principal town on the high plateau of southern Angola. He was at that moment talking to Victor Lobo, the man with whom Domingues and Marina were to spend the next six months.

'I wonder what kind of man he will be? I heard Comrade Zé say that we were getting an Anglo-Indian.'

'What on earth's an Anglo-Indian?'

'A sort of *mestiço*, I suppose, like you, Marina. Half English, half Indian.'

'Hmm, well I hope he speaks Portuguese.'

A buzzer sounded, the signal for the two Angolan girls to go into the Project Director's office. Zé made the introductions. He started in English as a sign of courtesy to his visitor. The words 'Good morning, this is Mr Lobo' exhausted his knowledge of English, and he changed to Portuguese with obvious relief.

'*Bom dia, bemvenido em Lubango, Doctor*. Good morning, welcome to Lubango, sir,' the girls said in chorus. Victor was surprised to hear himself addressed as 'Doctor', since he was only a simple transport engineer. He learned later that it was a title of honour given by the Angolans to all the experts who had come to help with the rebuilding of their war-torn country.

30   Victor smiled at them. 'So, you two will be my assistants. Well, I'm sure we will get along very well together.'

'We shall try to be good workers for *o Doctor*, and learn quickly what he has to teach us,' replied Domingues. She liked him. He spoke a simple, direct Portuguese, and he had kind
35   eyes. Best of all, he spoke to them as equals, which was not always the case with these foreign *cooperantes*.

Victor soon learned how lucky he was to have Domingues and Marina as his team. They worked hard for him, setting up interviews with officials who did not really want to see him, and
40   squeezing information out of a difficult bureaucratic system.

About two months after Victor's arrival, Zé Ribeiro called Domingues and Marina into his office. He explained to them that *o Doctor* wished to go down to the coast, to the port of Namibe City, to see what was left of the road and rail links
45   between the port and the interior. It meant a three-hour drive on a road which would take them from the pleasant climate of the high plateau, through the mists of the wild, wooded escarpment, and down, steeply and quickly, into the Namibe desert, a lonely place, inhabited by hard, unfriendly people.

50   They left early in the morning, in Zé's Toyota Landcruiser. Victor was glad to get away from the Gran Hotel d'Huila, with its awful food and its noisy army officers on leave from the front. He was really looking forward to the peace and tranquillity of the desert. As they left the escarpment and started across the
55   road through the desert, the contrast between the cool morning breeze up on the plateau and the baking heat of the desert was striking. Already, two hours after dawn, the sun was very powerful, and Victor could feel the sweat trickling down his body. Zé concentrated on driving, for the road had many pot-
60   holes. Marina chattered incessantly. Domingues said very little.

Her eyes seemed to be fixed on the landscape. There was some sparse vegetation, in places quite dense, but otherwise the landscape was featureless.

'What are you looking at, Domingues?' Marina asked impatiently, realising that Domingues was not really listening to her.

'Oh, nothing. Just looking.'

Victor interrupted. 'Who are those people?' he asked, pointing to small groups of men and women lining the roadside. They were very thin, their bony faces made more stark by their high cheekbones and domed foreheads. They were dressed in rags, thin blankets round their waists. Some of them carried sticks, presumably to control the herds of goats which milled around their legs. 'Look at their skin!' he went on. 'It's so . . . so shiny!' He stopped short of saying that it was blacker than any skin he had ever seen in Africa, so black that it was almost purple. 'It looks as if they've rubbed oil on themselves.'

'Oh, they're just a local tribe,' Domingues said in a very offhand way. 'The sun is so hot and the air is so dry here that they have to protect their skin. They rub it with an oil which they get from a plant that grows here in the desert. That's why their skin looks so black.'

Victor looked again at the faces of these rough desert people. Where had he seen such faces before, all bones and shiny skin? Of course! Domingues! Her skin was just like theirs, and her face had the same bone structure. He was on the point of asking her a question, but thought better of it.

The party eventually arrived at Namibe City, hot and tired and thirsty. The official who was supposed to have organised everything for the visit was away. They found only a young assistant, who was obviously very embarrassed. Yes, he had heard something about a transport expert. No, he knew nothing more. Victor realised that the situation had all the makings of a disaster: nothing had been arranged, and the visit was likely to be a waste of time. Africans!

67

'Look, Zé,' he said, making sure that the young assistant could hear his words, 'clearly nothing has been arranged for us. Could you make sure that we get something to eat and, above all, something to drink, right away. Then, if he' – indicating the young assistant – 'can take us to the docks and to the old railway station afterwards, our visit will not have been completely in vain. Oh yes, and check if there are any rooms for us in the local hotel – if there *is* a hotel in Namibe.' Domingues, who had remained silent, noted the deference in the young man's manner as soon as Victor started speaking. It was as if they were still in the colonial era: the white man commands and the black man obeys.

It was as Victor suspected: no drinks; no food; no hotel rooms. He felt himself getting angrier and angrier, his temper made worse by the heat and by his thirst. He was beginning to feel the first symptoms of dehydration, and knew how dangerous it was to lose so much body fluid. The young assistant led them to a verandah behind the office building. At least there was an awning where they could stay cool. The party sat at a table, silent. The young man brought a carafe of water and four dirty glasses.

'No beer? No pepsi-cola? No orange juice?' Victor asked.

'*Lamento!* I'm sorry!' replied the young man. He gave what seemed like a little bow and disappeared.

Victor looked at the water. It had a sort of brownish tinge to it, as if it contained sand. There is a rule in places like this: do not drink the water unless it has been filtered. You never know what organisms, what dangerous African microbes, might be lurking in such water. The other three, their African stomachs used to African microbes, filled their glasses and sipped gratefully at the lukewarm discoloured liquid.

'*O doctor não bebe*? Aren't you drinking, sir?' asked Domingues. Poor man, she thought. He looks quite ill. She poured him a glass and offered it to him, the expression on her face showing her concern for him.

Uttering a silent prayer, Victor took the glass and sipped the water. It had an unpleasant smell, but it tasted all right. He took another sip, and another, and another, until he felt quite uncomfortable with the amount of liquid washing around in his stomach. 135

The young man reappeared, carrying a tray with some tired-looking bread rolls on it. There was one for each of them. Zé wolfed his down; Domingues and Marina nibbled on theirs; and Victor, having inspected his, began to chew on it, noting its resemblance to wood and thinking how foolish he had been to 140 curse the food in his Lubango hotel: anything – even the terrible dried cod of the Gran Hotel d'Huila – was better than this. Having finished this bread-and-water meal, the four climbed back into the Toyota and made their way, first to the harbour, and then to what was left of the railway station. As he had 145 suspected, the road and rail systems between the coast and the interior had all but collapsed.

'Come on, it will be dark in an hour. Time we were getting back!' Victor said to Zé. Victor had had enough of Namibe City, and was anxious to get back to his hotel in Lubango before nine 150 o'clock, which was when they stopped serving dinner. By the time they approached the escarpment, it was already dark. They passed the place where the goat people had been that morning, but saw no one. The whole world seemed deserted. Victor looked at his watch. Zé seemed to be driving very slowly. Could 155 he get back to the hotel in time for dinner? There was a hollow feeling in Victor's stomach, almost a pain, that told him he was very hungry. The journey began to seem endless, especially since the party had fallen as silent as the African night around them. To take his mind off his stomach, Victor turned to 160 Domingues.

'*Falemos um boucado em ingles*? Why don't we try a little conversation in English?' he asked. Domingues was delighted. She knew very little, and was keen to learn more.

'Yes, please!' she said. She spoke the words in English, very 165

slowly but in an accent which was not unpleasant. He started
by telling her that he wanted to get back to the hotel before nine
o'clock so that he would be in time for dinner.

'We usually have fish and potatoes or a salad. Then, we
usually have some fruit,' he said, speaking slowly and clearly.

'What will you and Marina have for dinner tonight?'

'We have some beans.'

He wished he hadn't asked the question.

She paused to find the right words. 'Tonight . . . for dinner,
we shall have a soup of beans.'

'Bean soup. That's nice,' he said. The words sounded hollow.

There was a longer pause this time before she added: 'If there
is water.'

The last four words stopped Victor in his tracks. The water
supply in Lubango was, like everything else, unreliable, but he
found it difficult to take in the reality of these young girls' lives.
Their dinner would be just a simple bean soup, and that only
if they had some clean water in the house. His dinner at the
hotel was a feast by comparison. His stomach was aching quite
badly by the time they reached Lubango, and he spent little
time saying goodbye to his three companions. He rushed into
the hotel restaurant and was in time, but only just in time, to
get the main course – the predicted piece of tasteless dried cod
– with a salad of sorts, and, to make the meal more civilised,
a bottle of rough red wine. He ate and drank quickly, as if he
were afraid that someone might take his food and drink away
before he had finished, and went straight to his room. He lay
on his bed without undressing, feeling very queer inside. The
fish? The wine? Something was wrong. His stomach still ached.
He was sweating profusely. He looked at the ceiling, at the
flaking plaster, the slow decay, the signs of neglect everywhere,
the signs of breakdown. What was he doing here? What could
he hope to achieve here in this poor, confused country? Pains
shot through his belly, making him cry out.

In their cramped little room, Domingues and Marina were

asleep. The bean soup had been good, but, as usual, there had not been enough of it. Somewhere, far below the plateau, a thin old woman squatted by the side of the road keeping watch over her goats. Her purple-black skin gleamed in the moonlight. She wrapped a blanket round her shoulders to keep out the cold of the desert night.

Victor shivered and pulled a blanket up over his body. At once he had to throw it off as the sweating began again. He cried out in terror at the pain growing inside him. The terrible microbe was taking effect. His belly began to swell horribly, like a balloon, and his temperature soared to a hundred and three. Just before he lost consciousness, he remembered Domingues and he remembered the goat people with their shining skin and their bony faces. And he remembered, last of all, Domingues's words in her halting English: 'We shall have a soup of beans . . . if there is water.'

Glossary and Language Practice

Mangiarotti

GLOSSARY

starving to death (line 2): an exaggerated way of saying 'very hungry'.

my money had run out (line 6): I had no money left.

high and low (line 20): everywhere.

tramping (line 20): not simply walking, but walking a long way and for a long time.

peering (line 21): looking, but 'peering' suggests that it was dark, or that it was not easy to see things down the side streets.

passers-by (line 21): with most compound nouns, the last part of the compound shows the plural: for example, bedroom – bedrooms; policeman – policemen. 'Passer-by' is an exception, as are words ending in '-in-law' describing relatives by marriage: son-in-law – sons-in-law.

in vain (line 23): without success; without any useful result.

a second-hand dealer (line 25): a man who buys and sells goods which are not new.

I'd better (line 28–9): an idiomatic expression meaning 'The best thing for me to do is to . . .' The ''d' is short for 'had'.

for goodness' sake! (line 30–31): usually an expression of protest. Similarly: 'For heaven's sake!' and, not always acceptable, 'For God's sake!'

what if (line 33): what would happen if . . .

were (line 33): 'were' is often used instead of 'was' (If I were; If he/she/it were) in conditionals which describe an imagined situation: for example, 'If I were you, I wouldn't do that.'

red-haired and fair-skinned (line 33): with red hair and having fair skin.

Talk about. . . ! (line 35): a fixed expression to comment on something which is difficult, shocking, amazing, etc.

looking for a needle in a haystack (line 35): trying to find something which it is almost impossible to find. The usual pattern is: 'It is/was like looking for a needle in a haystack.'

All the same (line 35): in spite of that.

there was nothing for it but to (line 36): it was my only choice; I could not do anything else.

I happened to look (line 39–40): 'happen to' something suggests that your action was not intentional: it just happened.

Why on earth. . . ? (line 68): the words 'on earth' after a question word are used to emphasise your surprise, anger, etc.

Was he showing off? (line 69): 'showing off' is a childish and unattractive way of letting other people know how clever, rich, successful, etc., you are.

Oh, come on (line 93): a fixed expression used in conversation. It usually means: 'Don't try to deceive me'; 'Don't try to avoid the point'.

I was only pulling your leg (line 94): I was only teasing you, making fun of you.

I liked to think of myself as (line 96–7): 'I liked to think that I was . . .'

As for your shoes . . . ! (line 107): 'as for' is used to introduce an item in a series, and suggests that you are going to say something critical about it.

Ugh! (line 114): a sound which people make when they see or hear something which they find unpleasant.

I couldn't help admiring (line 117): the expression 'help doing' is always used with 'can't', 'cannot' or 'couldn't'.

worked out (line 118): deduced.

Sherlock Holmes (line 119): a fictional detective created by Sir Arthur Conan Doyle.

upshot (line 123): final result.

After all, . . . (line 125–6): 'After all', used at the beginning of a sentence, means: 'What is important . . .'; 'What really matters

74

. . .' Used at the end of a sentence, as in *So you got to Paris after all, eh?* (line 133), it means: 'in the end'; 'finally'.

everything had turned out well (line 127): everything was finally all right, in spite of difficulties earlier on.

took over the conversation (line 131): Silvano did not wait for Chris to finish speaking. Instead, he started talking.

Good for you! (line 133): an expression of congratulation, like 'Well done!'

guy (line 134): a slang expression for 'man'. In the plural, 'guys' may refer to a mixed group of males and females.

to get in touch with him (line 136–7): to contact him, by letter, phone, etc.

he's sort of half-expecting you, Joe (line 137): 'sort of' shows that the following word or expression is not exact.

Why don't you . . . ? (line 137–8): a question in form, but it is really a suggestion.

Oh, yes, I had found him all right (line 140): in this case, 'all right' does not mean: 'without difficulty'; it means: 'certainly', 'without any doubt'.

LANGUAGE PRACTICE

A

Replace the words underlined with an expression from the text based on the word given in brackets. Make any necessary grammatical changes.

Example: He suddenly started to laugh (burst).
          He burst out laughing.

1 I was very, very hungry (death).
2 I needed a week to get from Milan to Paris (take).
3 Don't be angry. I was only making fun of you (leg).
4 I looked everywhere for my pen (high).
5 Let's have a picnic (Why . . . ?).
6 I'm afraid I don't speak French very well (not good).
7 His stare seemed to penetrate me (through).

8 He switched <u>continually</u> from one subject to another (keep).

9 I <u>knew</u> from his complexion that he had been sunbathing (tell).

10 <u>It was impossible for me not to</u> notice her ear-rings (help).

B

Supply the missing words. In each case, the first letter of the missing word is given. All these expressions are taken from the text.

1 He s_____ his shoulders, as if to say that it didn't m_____ to him w_____ I stayed or went away.

2 She always wore too much jewellery: it was her way of s_____ o_____.

3 He roared with l_____: he f_____ the situation so funny.

4 I knew that her office was near the Town Hall. I searched for hours, but it was l_____ looking for a n_____ in a h_____.

5 We had some problems, but everything t_____ o_____ fine in the end.

C

Questions for discussion.

1 If you had to describe Mangiarotti to someone else, what could you say about (a) his appearance; (b) his character; (c) his age? Is he married?

2 The story is set in 1960. Can you still tell young people's nationality from their appearance nowadays? What about older people? Describe a person of a particular nationality and see if others can identify him/her.

3 If you had to describe the narrator to someone else, what could you say about (a) his appearance; (b) his previous history; (c) his character?

Glossary and Language Practice

The Invisible Man

GLOSSARY

would make a fuss (line 6): would be angry or annoyed.

speck (line 6): a small, unwanted mark, as in 'a speck of dust'.

with a sharp tongue (line 8): who would quickly express his anger.

telling me to mind my own business (line 17–18): telling me that it was nothing to do with me, that it was not my concern.

screeched to a stop (line 22–3): 'screech' describes the sound of the wheels on the road. Compare *squeal of tyres* (line 14–15).

staring straight ahead. I followed his gaze (line 24): 'staring' and 'gazing' are ways of looking at something or someone for a long time. Usually, 'staring' is rude – you are angry or curious; 'gazing' is not rude – you are full of love, admiration or wonder.

alongside it (line 25–6): 'alongside' gives the idea of two things being parallel.

bobbed up (line 30): suddenly appeared above the surface. We use the verb 'bob' to describe the movement of a light object, such as a cork, on water.

It dawned on me (line 35): I gradually realised. The image is of the sun rising at dawn.

I was supposed to follow him (line 39): he expected me to follow him. Note the passive construction: he expected me to → I was expected to.

My curiosity got the better of me (line 40): my curiosity was so strong that I had to satisfy it.

standing upright (line 47): not bending forward or leaning.

clutching (line 54): holding it tightly so as not to lose or drop it.

had seen better days (line 57): a fixed expression to describe something old and worn out, but which is still in use.

bundled him into the back of the car (line 64–5): 'bundled' suggests that the old man was pushed or thrown into the car as if he were a bundle or parcel.

stuck out his tongue (line 76): a rude gesture, usually made by children.

patted his briefcase (line 77): touching his briefcase lightly and repeatedly.

the thought crossed my mind (line 80): similar to 'it occurred to me'; it describes the way you suddenly think of an idea or an explanation but without necessarily accepting it as true.

a fair question (line 89): a reasonable, acceptable question.

dying to (line 90): wanting very much to.

show him a thing or two (line 96–7): an idiomatic expression meaning that you will make someone respect you by doing something clever or amazing.

for all the world (line 99): totally; completely.

as mad as a hatter (line 102): completely mad. Compare *off his head* (line 180).

when he's not around (line 103): when he's not present.

humouring him (line 105): trying to please him by saying what he wanted to hear.

let alone pasta (line 124): 'let alone' is used to say that one thing is even harder to accept than another. 'She can't even stand up, let alone walk.'

herbs (line 132): plants with good qualities, used in medicine, cooking, etc.

it could have done with (line 140–41): it would have been improved if he had added . . .

loosens the tongue (line 143–4): makes people relax and talk.

off his head (line 180): mad.

that's the beauty of it (line 182): that is what makes it such a great idea.

a banner headline (line 185): a headline in very big letters on the front page of popular newspapers.

keep a straight face (line 202–3): not laugh when you really want to.

let the old man down (line 210): disappoint or betray the old man by revealing his secret to his son.

will be off again to that damned ditch collecting herbs (line 220–21): he will go back to the ditch and he will start collecting herbs there.

damned (line 221) and *bloody* (line 222): swear-words. 'Damned' is now regarded as mild and acceptable by most people; 'bloody' is not.

looked across to me (line 225): the preposition 'to', rather than the usual 'at', gives the idea of co-operation, of including the other person. Compare: 'She threw the ball to me' (including); and 'she threw a stone at me' (excluding).

The smile . . . was a picture (line 227–8): the smile was a wonderful
thing to see, like a picture in an art gallery.

LANGUAGE PRACTICE

A

*Replace the words underlined with an expression from the text based on the
word(s) given in brackets. Make any necessary grammatical changes.*

Example: He <u>suddenly started to laugh</u> (burst).
           He burst out laughing.

1 He <u>got angry</u> because we had forgotten our keys (fuss).
2 I <u>couldn't imagine</u> why he was so angry (slightest).
3 She made it clear that it was <u>nothing to do with me</u> (business).
4 A movement in the garden <u>attracted my attention</u> (eye).
5 His clothes <u>were of good quality but very old</u> (better days).
6 An idea <u>suddenly occurred to me</u> (cross).
7 The old fellow was <u>completely crazy</u> (hatter).
8 He <u>easily</u> found what he was looking for (no difficulty).
9 I found it very hard <u>not to start laughing</u> (straight face).
10 I <u>badly needed</u> something to drink (die).

B

*Supply the missing words. In each case, the first letter(s) of the missing word
is (are) given. All these expressions are taken from the text.*

1 Get this place t_____ u_____ right away.
2 He was in front of me, so I had to run to c_____ u_____
   with him.
3 He spoke so quietly that I had to l_____ f_____ to hear what
   he said.
4 The road ran a_____ the river for several miles before turning
   off.
5 John has a quick temper and a very s_____ tongue.

6 It is rude to s_____ your t_____ out at people.

7 The dog held the bone in its teeth, and refused to l_____
   g_____ of it.

8 He doesn't know what he's talking about: t_____ no n_____
   of him.

9 The dog ran a_____, and I was sent to f_____ it
   b_____.

10 She cl_____ her purse tightly so as not to dr_____ it.

C

Questions for discussion.

1 How would you describe to someone else (a) the old man's physical
   appearance; (b) his past history; (c) his character?

2 How does Mangiarotti feel about his father? What incidents in the
   story show his impatience with his father?

3 How does the narrator's attitude to the old man change during the
   course of the story? Describe to someone else how you would react
   in the same circumstances.

Gossip

GLOSSARY

as it were (line 10): 'as it were' shows that the preceding words, 'share
   himself out', are used with a special meaning.

give me a hand to (line 17–18): help me to. Similarly: *a helping hand*
   (line 65–6).

I'm a bit fed up myself (line 22): *fed up* (colloquial): completely bored
   or unhappy with your situation; 'myself' is added to contrast with
   'you' in the previous sentence; that is: *you* may be all right, but *I*
   am fed up.'

To tell you the truth . . . (line 22–3): announces that you are saying
   something very frank and honest.

row (line 23): (pronounced [rau]) a quarrel.

all rolled into one (line 26–7): an idiom meaning that someone or something has several different functions at the same time.

in the company of (line 35): in their presence; with them. Contrast the use of 'company' in the sense of a business: *the insurance company* (line 103).

on the whole (line 37): in general; for the most part.

put the colour back into your cheeks (line 50): a fixed expression to describe a medicine, a treat, etc., that will make you feel better.

had your hair done (line 51): 'done' is used here as an all-purpose word to include shampooing, setting, perming, waving, tinting and all the other amazing things that women do (or have done) to their hair.

overdoing things a bit (line 53): working or trying too hard.

I wish I had talent (line 55): when we wish for something imagined or unreal, the tenses used after it are either past (for example: 'I wish I had – but I haven't'), or conditional (for example: I wish I could fly – but I can't).

too wrapped up in themselves (line 61–2): too concerned about their own lives to care about anyone else.

a chat (line 65): a friendly talk, usually about nothing important.

tongues began to wag (line 67–8): people began to spread gossip and scandal.

propped up (line 68): put into a leaning position.

leads him on (line 77): encourages him to do something wrong.

have a quiet word with (line 87): speak to him privately.

were made aware (line 89): 'were made aware' is used rather than 'became aware' to emphasise that someone made it his or her business to let the husbands know what was going on.

a roving eye (line 93): a man with a roving eye spends a lot of time looking at women and assessing their sexual availability.

a stray dog (line 94): a dog without a home; one that is not under control.

sulky (line 95): 'sulking' is the typical reaction of a child when it cannot have what it wants, and is characterised by an angry expression on the face, a refusal to talk, and the forward projection of the bottom lip.

began . . . to drop hints (line 96): began to say things, but in an indirect
way, to cause people to become aware of the situation.

offhand (line 97): casual. The husbands did not want their wives to
think that they were really worried.

want to have their way (line 98): want to serve their own interests.

before long (line 106): soon; after a short time.

clucked (line 107): made a self-satisfied noise, like the one made by a
hen that has just laid an egg.

walked out on her husband (line 114): left him.

LANGUAGE PRACTICE

A

*Replace the words underlined with an expression from the text based on the
word(s) given in brackets. Make any necessary grammatical changes.*

Example: He suddenly started to laugh (burst).
He burst out laughing.

1 Please listen carefully to what I am saying (attention).
2 You must ignore her (notice).
3 I wonder if you could help me (hand)?
4 John and his wife aren't speaking to each other: they've quarrelled
again (another row).
5 We can hardly wait to see you all again (forward).
6 Everyone was very glad when he left the village (sigh of relief).
7 Fred prefers to be with women (company).
8 Children sulk if they cannot get what they want (way).
9 As a matter of fact, I'm feeling rather tired (truth).
10 He's too concerned about himself to care about anyone else
(wrapped).

Glossary and Language Practice

B

Supply the missing words. In most cases, the first letter of the missing word is given. All these expressions are taken from the text.

1 Thank you for your help. I a_____ it very much.

2 They say that Audrey has w_____ out o_____ her husband. Is it true, or is it just a r_____ that's going r_____?

3 Have a drink of this. It'll soon put the c_____ b_____ into your c_____!

4 Would you like a cup of tea. I've just p_____ the kettle o_____.

5 Please c_____ r_____ on us the next time you're in town.

6 She didn't warn me she was leaving. She just w_____ o_____ o_____ me one day.

7 Everyone trusts her; that's why everyone confides _____ her.

8 They complimented him _____ his success in the examinations.

9 You look worn out. Are you sure you haven't been o_____ things a b_____?

10 I've had enough of this. I'm really f_____ u_____ with it.

C

Questions for discussion.

1 We are told very little about Fred Battersby's history, except that he is a widower. Try to think of reasons why he got on so well with women. What was his childhood like? His parents? His wife? Did he have any children?

2 What was Fred's importance to his married ladies? In what way, do you think, were they important to him?

3 Mrs Somersham was the one who started the gossip about Fred. Why did she do this, do you think? What makes people gossip? Was Mr Somersham also a gossip in your view? What were his reasons for 'having a quiet word' with one of the husbands?

4 This story is set in a village. Could such things happen in a big town?

Crash

GLOSSARY

on tiptoe (line 5): on the tips or points of one's toes.

before impact (line 21): before hitting another object.

prod (line 29): to poke with the end of the finger.

I don't mind at all (line 33): 'at all' after 'not' emphasises the negative.

They mean me no harm (line 34): they do not intend to harm me. Similarly: *they do not mean to hurt me* (line 38–9).

it does not mist over (line 47–8): usually when you breathe on a mirror, your breath condenses on the cold glass like a mist.

test for vampires (line 48): test to see if someone is a vampire.

a dozen (line 49): literally, 'twelve', but here it means 'a number of', 'several'.

Let's try a name (line 51): say a name, any name, and see what happens.

chatter (line 53): 'chatter' refers to unimportant, even silly, talk.

shakes his head (line 56): to indicate 'no'.

childish (line 66) and *childlike* (line 67): 'childish' describes the bad qualities of a child, for example, immaturity, unreasonableness, selfishness; 'childlike', simply means 'like a child', 'innocent'.

If only (line 72): everything would be all right if . . .

think back to (line 83): recall; try to remember.

faded (line 87): as the light fades (grows less) towards sunset, it becomes more difficult to see colours.

I can just make out a table (line 87–8): I can just manage to identify a table.

plump (line 90): pleasantly fat.

day-dreaming (line 94): thinking and enjoying pleasant thoughts to the extent that you are no longer aware of your surroundings. Some students can day-dream while appearing to be paying attention to their teacher – a wonderful gift.

face-down (line 103–4): lying on my stomach.

cry myself to sleep (line 104): cry until I fall asleep.

afraid to open my eyes (line 108–9): afraid of what I might see if I open my eyes. Compare *afraid of the lights* (line 115).

coming round (line 110): regaining consciousness after, for example, fainting, being under anaesthetic, being in a coma.

was used to being (line 113): in expressions like 'be/get used to', 'be/get accustomed to', the word 'to' is a preposition, and must be followed by the gerund form, '-ing'.

you've made it (line 123): you've survived; you've recovered.

head to toe (line 131): completely; covering the whole body.

LANGUAGE PRACTICE

A

Replace the words underlined with an expression from the text based on the word(s) given in brackets. Make any necessary grammatical changes.

Example: He suddenly started to laugh (burst).
          He burst out laughing.

1   It doesn't bother me (mind).

2   It was clear that she was the boss (charge).

3   I wish I were taller (only/short).

4   They wanted to see if he had diabetes (test).

5   It looks as if he is regaining consciousness (come).

6   It's no problem for me to walk to work every day (used).

7   She lay on her stomach (face).

8   They do not intend to hurt me (mean/harm).

9   I want you to be completely honest with me (truth).

10 The shelf was so high that I had to stretch up as far as possible to reach it (tiptoe).

B

Supply the missing words. In each case, the first letter(s) of the missing word is (are) given. All these expressions are taken from the text.

1   Our house l_____ out o_____ t_____ the park.

2   I intend to f_____ o_____ who wrote this on the wall.

3   It was so dark that I could only just m_____ o_____ who she was.

4   Did you c_____ o_____ my instructions?

5 I don't approve o_____ noisy motorbikes: there o_____ to
   be a l_____ against them.
6 There was ice on the road, and I nearly l_____ c_____ of
   the car.
7 They were ch_____ away in a language I didn't know.
8 If o_____ I w_____ so old, I would marry you tomorrow!
9 I've told you a d_____ times not to call me Fatty.
10 My eyelids feel as h_____ as l_____. I can hardly keep my
   eyes open.

C

Questions for discussion.

1 Can you now explain exactly what happened to the person in the
   story? What do you know about that person's sex, name and
   physical appearance?
2 Tell someone else about a really strange or peculiar event. It may
   be something that really happened to you, or it may be imaginary.
   Tell it as well as you can, and see if they can decide whether it is
   true or made up.
3 What is day-dreaming? How, why and when does it happen? Give
   some examples of your own day-dreaming.

Magic

GLOSSARY

It looks out of place (line 3): it doesn't belong; it looks odd.
sleek (line 3): long and smooth and elegant.
came to be (line 5): was; 'came to be' expresses surprise that it was
   there.
he took to drink (line 15–16): he began to drink heavily.
took it over (line 22): took possession of it.

You mean . . . (line 24): expresses disbelief: 'Are you seriously telling me that . . .?'

Squat (line 35): very short and fat; 'squatting' is a way of sitting on your heels like a frog.

Stumpy (line 35): like the broken-off or sawn-off stumps of tree trunks.

before my time (line 38): before I came here; before I was born.

mate (line 38): a colloquial expression for 'friend'; a familiar way of addressing another man.

prompted (line 42): in the theatre, the prompter is the person who whispers the words to an actor who has forgotten his lines.

another soul (line 48): any other person.

grown-ups (line 61): a children's word for adults.

call her names (line 63): call her rude names.

properly (line 68): no one had had a really good look at it.

carvings (line 69): symbolic or artistic marks made with a sharp instrument.

beware of (line 70): be careful, as in 'Beware of the dog'.

cross your fingers (line 73): a gesture for ensuring luck or success.

a spell (line 75): magic words which cause things to happen.

kids (line 83): a slang expression for 'children'; a kid is a young goat.

to make matters worse (line 93): a fixed expression; here it means: 'It was bad enough that he had a long thin body and a small head, etc., but, what was even worse . . .'

a thing or two (line 96): an idiom, emphasising how much he knows.

Cockle, his name is . . . (line 97): the barman puts first the idea that is in the front of his mind, then finishes the sentence. Similarly: *A growth in her throat, it was* (line 217). Notice too how the barman misses out the subject pronoun: *Used to be . . .* (line 98); *Spent all his time . . .* (line 198).

an old-timer (line 100): a pioneer, who was there in the early days.

coaxing (line 102): gently persuading, without causing resistance.

she let go (line 123): she released his hand.

a police sergeant no less (line 129): nothing less important than a police sergeant, and so a very important man. The tone is, of course, ironic.

He did mention it to his wife (line 131): 'did' is stressed. The form do/does/did + base verb (for example, 'he does smoke' for 'he smokes') is used when you want to make a contrast with or contradict something that has been said to you.

though (line 131): at the end of a sentence, 'though' modifies a previous sentence, and is similar to 'but': 'He said he'd help us. He didn't, though.' (He said he'd help us, but he didn't.)

But she went all the same (line 138–9): she went in spite of her fear.

You're Cockle's woman (line 141): correctly and politely, she should have said, 'wife'.

spread like wildfire (line 149): very quickly, like fire in a dry area.

Hippocrates (line 159–60): a Greek physician, the father of medicine (*c.* 460 BC–*c.* 370 BC).

Reader's Digest (line 160): a magazine which provides instant wisdom by giving short easy-to-read summaries of scientific and other information.

hey presto (line 166–7): the words which magicians say to announce the result of their magic, for example, when producing a rabbit from a hat.

a magical flower (line 181–2): a real flower which is so wonderful that it is 'like magic'. A 'magic flower' is not a real flower, but the product of magic.

weeping (line 183): crying, with emphasis on the flow of tears.

the fact of the matter is (line 194): 'the truth is . . . '

practically moved in with her (line 195–6): went to live with her. The word 'practically' means that 'moved in' is almost but not exactly what he did.

It hardly bears thinking about (line 196–7): a fixed expression; the barman finds the idea of love between Dan and Martha so disgusting that he doesn't even like to think about it. Compare *The idea . . . was too much to swallow* (line 208–10).

choked to death (line 218): died because her throat was blocked.

lay uncared for (line 227): the same pattern as 'stand still', etc.: 'lie' (VERB) + 'uncared for' (ADJECTIVE).

A thought struck me (line 231): similar to 'a thought crossed my mind', but 'strike' gives an idea of the power or suddenness of the idea.

sneered (line 240): 'to sneer' is to make a facial expression with lips unpleasantly downturned; it is often accompanied by a short noise to show contempt, cynical disbelief, etc.

. . . my eye! (line 241): an idiomatic way of saying that you believe something to be not just untrue, but complete rubbish.

Glossary and Language Practice

LANGUAGE PRACTICE

A

Replace the words underlined with an expression from the text based on the word given in brackets. Make any necessary grammatical changes.

Example: He suddenly started to laugh (burst).
           He burst out laughing.

1   I walked for miles without meeting anyone at all (soul).
2   He didn't feel like going to the opera, but I gently persuaded him to come with me (coax).
3   We settled down in a small country town after the war (home).
4   Just as I was leaving, I suddenly thought of something (strike).
5   Why don't you ask Joe? He could tell you a great deal about the subject (two).
6   I no longer believe in orthodox medicine (faith).
7   The old settee looked strange among all the modern furniture (place).
8   I'm quite certain that she is a witch (doubt).
9   I found it easy to get him to talk (difficulty).
10 I didn't want my dinner, but I ate it anyway (same).

B

Supply the missing words. In each case, the first letter(s) of the missing word is (are) given. All these expressions are taken from the text.

1   The taxi lay empty until Martha t_____ it o_____.
2   After he became a widower, Dan practically m_____ in w_____ Martha.
3   Don't let him kiss you: you might t_____ i_____ a frog!
4   Children can believe in magic, but gr_____ should k_____ b_____.
5   I've got a test tomorrow, so k_____ your f_____ cr_____!

89

6 I cleaned the engine, but I still f_____ to g_____ it st_____.

7 The rumour about the gold s_____ like w_____ through the town.

8 Children didn't like her, so they c_____ her n_____.

9 He swallowed a fishbone and nearly ch_____ to d_____.

10 I don't remember airships: they were long b_____ my t_____.

C

Questions for discussion.

1 What theories were there about Martha's miraculous cures? Tell someone your own opinion, and see if he/she agrees with you.

2 If you had to describe the barman to someone else, how would you describe (a) his physical appearance; (b) his character; (c) his attitude to the events in Martha Gooby's life?

3 What kind of man was Dan Cockle in your view? Discuss with someone else what he and Martha meant to each other.

A Spray of Heather

GLOSSARY

spray (title): a piece with several small branches.

try his luck (line 26): see if he could succeed or win.

brought the conversation round (line 26–7): cleverly changed the subject of conversation to something he wanted to talk about.

give his lecture a miss (line 32): a colloquial way of saying 'miss his lecture', 'not bother to go to it'.

stuffy (line 34): airless, and therefore hot and unpleasant.

sneak off (line 35): go away, making sure that no one notices.

his heart sank (line 37): he felt a sudden disappointment.

Glossary and Language Practice

weaving his way (line 42): you cannot simply go in a straight line as you walk along a crowded pavement: you have to 'weave' – keep moving from side to side – to avoid bumping into people.

putting a brave face on it (line 45): as he couldn't avoid it, he made it appear that he would actually enjoy it.

strolling (line 60): a slow, easy, pleasant and essentially aimless way of walking.

Where there's a will, there's a way (line 71–2): a proverb, meaning 'If you really want to do something badly enough, you will find a way to do it'.

cobble-stones (line 73): rounded stones, pretty to look at, but hard to walk on.

got themselves happily lost (line 74): they soon got lost, but, as they were not going anywhere in particular, they didn't mind being lost.

muddled (line 77): confused.

well-meaning (line 94): having good intentions.

buffeted (line 97): violently pushed, knocked.

did not allow for (line 105): did not consider the needs of.

lent a hand (line 109): helped.

whining (line 126): an unpleasant, demanding sound made by children who want something they know they cannot have.

root (line 133): search for, the word suggests the difficulty of trying to find something small in a deep pocket.

turned on (line 135): attacked.

crippled (line 139–40): we prefer to avoid direct words like 'crippled' nowadays, but to use expressions like 'physically handicapped' or 'disabled' instead. The gypsy, not being a member of polite society, used the old-fashioned word.

used up (line 143): used them until there were none left.

swear-word (line 143): swear-words are usually profanities or refer to certain bodily organs and functions which polite society does not wish to talk about.

snatched (line 146): the word suggests the violence with which she removed the spray of heather from his lapel.

LANGUAGE PRACTICE

A

Replace the words underlined with an expression from the text based on the word(s) given in brackets. Make any necessary grammatical changes.

Example: He <u>suddenly started to laugh</u> (burst).
He burst out laughing.

1 <u>Why don't we</u> have a look round the town (let)?
2 We decided <u>not to bother to go to</u> the lecture (give/miss).
3 It may be difficult, but <u>we should at least</u> try (harm).
4 <u>There's no point in</u> waiting any longer (waste).
5 <u>Everyone remained absolutely silent</u> (word).
6 I don't usually gamble, but I decided to <u>see if I could win</u> at roulette (luck).
7 As he couldn't get out of taking Andrew, he decided to <u>make the best of</u> it (brave/face).
8 <u>Confidentially</u>, I think she's a liar (between).
9 Someone <u>approached</u> me and asked me for money (up).
10 I <u>didn't enjoy</u> having to walk home in the rain (no fun).

B

Supply the missing words. In each case, the first letter(s) of the missing word is (are) given. All these expressions are taken from the text.

1 When you do a good d_____, you f_____ really good i_____.
2 My h_____ s_____ when I realised it was my t_____ to give a speech.
3 We went for a st_____ through the old town to do some s_____.
4 There was total confusion until Maria arrived and t_____ ch_____ of the situation.
5 There were no taxis, so I had to walk a_____ the w_____ b_____ to the hotel.

6 You can do anything if you really want to: where there's a w_____, there's a w_____.

7 When a gypsy is angry, she will c_____ you terrible n_____ and use a lot of sw_____ words and c_____s.

8 We started by talking about politics, but Henry soon b_____ the conversation r_____ to his favourite topic: girls.

C

Questions for discussion.

1 If you had to describe Andrew to someone else, what could you say about (a) his physical appearance; (b) his character; (c) his professional background?

2 Describe Tony's feelings when he first realised that he had to accompany Andrew. Do you think his attitude changed by the time the day was over? What events and incidents made the biggest impression on him?

3 Explain to someone else your opinion of the gypsy's attitude and behaviour. How do you think her reaction to a person in a wheel-chair differs from (a) the taxi-driver's; (b) the barman's; (c) Tony's; (d) yours?

The Wrong Pig

GLOSSARY

as different as chalk and cheese (line 1): not in the least alike.

make himself understood (line 14): make sure that others could understand him.

chatting up (line 16): a slang expression, which describes the way a boy talks to a girl he has just met when he wants to impress her and persuade her to go out with him.

the latest girl (line 21) and *the last one* (line 21): 'latest' means most recent and *current*, while 'last' means last and *past*; the 'last' may or may not be followed by more.

every inch the (line 26): her behaviour and character were typical of . . .

held herself (line 28–9): refers to the straight-backed, aristocratic way in which she stood and moved.

make up his mind (line 34): decide.

fell for (line 37): was attracted by.

a foursome (line 38): a group of four.

head over heels in love (line 42): madly in love.

tongue-tied (line 50): too shy or embarrassed to speak.

Never mind . . . (line 63): but it wasn't important because . . .

going through (line 68): suffering.

give her a hug (line 70–71): held her tightly but briefly in his arms.

to the point (line 79): to the subject that was really important to him.

at home (line 99): comfortable; relaxed.

on first name terms with (line 99–100): he knew them well enough to call them by their first names.

popping the question (line 102): asking someone to marry you; the expression is in inverted commas because it is a slightly humorous colloquial expression.

As it turned out (line 102): in view of what happened later.

greeted us like long lost friends (line 120): a fixed expression, meaning that he greeted us as if we were old friends of his.

sat us (line 121): put us; invited us to sit.

It takes all sorts to make a world (line 128): a proverb: every community ('a world') must have many different kinds ('sorts') of people.

a fancy-dress party (line 153): a party where everyone goes in costume ('fancy dress'), dressed up to look like someone or something else.

change the subject (line 156): talk about something different.

a couple of (line 158): literally, 'two', but sometimes used to mean 'a few'.

for a bet (line 160): Suzanne thinks that perhaps someone has bet them that they will not do it.

burst in (line 161): interrupted.

would never have dreamt of (line 168): it was completely against her nature and beliefs to speak to them.

You know perfectly well (line 175): don't pretend that you don't know.

stuffy (line 179): pompous; having no sense of humour.

going from bad to worse (line 180–81): becoming more and more unpleasant and difficult.

turning . . . sour (line 182): becoming unpleasant, uncomfortable.

take back (line 192): pretend that they had never said those things.

I kept out of the way (line 194): avoided them.

broke up (line 195): finished their relationship.

poured his heart out (line 197): told me everything that he was feeling.

he had brought it on himself (line 198–9): it was his own fault, the result of his own actions.

slaughter (line 215): pronounced [slautə].

LANGUAGE PRACTICE

A

Replace the words underlined with an expression from the text based on the word(s) given in brackets. Make any necessary grammatical changes.

Example: He suddenly started to laugh (burst).
            He burst out laughing.

1   He couldn't stop looking at them (eyes).
2   We enjoyed each other's company (on well).
3   We try to be hospitable: we like our guests to be relaxed when they visit us (home).
4   I couldn't decide whether to do maths or physics (mind).
5   We soon got to know them (acquaintance).
6   His cruel words really hurt me (through/knife).
7   I was very embarrassed so I tried to get everyone to talk about something else (change).
8   Nobody paid any attention to us (notice).
9   I thought that it was his own fault (bring/himself).
10 Suzanne is so shy that she would find it impossible to ask a boy for a dance (dream).

B

Supply the missing words. In each case, the first letter(s) of the missing word is (are) given. All these expressions are taken from the text.

1   The boss is very friendly: he is on first n_____ t_____ with all his staff.

2   Bruno f_____ head o_____ h_____ in love with Eveline.

3   He hadn't seen us for a long time, but he gr_____ us like l_____ l_____ friends.

4   My brother and I are not at all alike: we are as different as c_____ and c_____.

5   You could tell from the way she gave orders that she was e_____ i_____ the manager.

6   Tolerate other people: it t_____ all s_____ to m_____ a w_____.

7   Instead of getting better, t_____s just went f_____ bad to w_____.

8   He has no s_____ of humour: he just can't t_____ a j_____.

9   I spoke slowly in order to make m_____ u_____.

10 You didn't really f_____ f_____ his story about being a millionaire, did you?

C

Questions for discussion.

1   If you had to describe Bruno to someone else, what could you say about (a) his physical appearance; (b) his background; (c) his character? Do you think you would get on with him?

2   Can you explain Eveline's reaction to the odd couple in the restaurant? How do you react to people who are very different from you, or who are odd in some way? Which of the four characters (the narrator, Bruno, Eveline and Suzanne) are you closest to in this respect?

3   We are told very little about the narrator (the 'I' in this story). What can you say, or guess, about his physical appearance, background and character?

Wild Mushrooms

Note: As this story is set in Catalonia, Catalan spellings are used; for example, *Senyor, Senyora, Catalunya, Cristofol* (for Cristobal), etc.

GLOSSARY

species (line 4): the word is both singular and plural.

As far as the English are concerned (line 7–8): in the opinion of the English.

dreading (line 18): experiencing a terrible fear of a future event.

townies (line 33): an unkind word for people who live in towns.

at once (line 38): immediately; without delay.

Here we go again! (line 49): an expression generally used to express our dismay or annoyance at something which, in our opinion, happens much too often.

I-Spy (line 62): someone decides on an object which he or she can see. He or she then says: 'I spy with my little eye something beginning with [the first letter of the object]', and the others have to guess the object.

I won't be long (line 79): I'll be back soon.

All heads (line 89) and *All eyes* (line 91): dramatic ways of saying 'everyone'.

the most prized (line 96): the one that everybody wanted to find.

left clean plates (line 118): ate everything up.

tact (line 136): the quality of wishing to avoid hurting or offending people, exemplified by the story of the plumber who, going into a bathroom where a lady is having a bath, leaves at once with the words: 'I'm terribly sorry, sir'.

managed to get (line 137–8): he got them, but with some difficulty.

97

Wild Mushrooms and Other Very Short Stories

LANGUAGE PRACTICE

A

Replace the words underlined with an expression from the text based on the word(s) given in brackets. Make any necessary grammatical changes.

Example: He suddenly started to laugh (burst).
              He burst out laughing.

1   I'll be back soon (long).
2   Everybody looked at the bundle (eyes/turn).
3   The English believe that wild mushrooms are dangerous (concerned).
4   The children ate everything that was given to them (leave/plates).
5   They turned right at the end of the lane (hand).
6   She decided to make the best of a bad situation (face on it).
7   They were still eating their soup when he returned (half way).
8   There was a wooded hillside through the window (look out).
9   My doctor says that fungi are valuable plants (according).
10 They can go by themselves (own).

B

Supply the missing words. In each case, the first letter(s) of the missing word is (are) given. All these expressions are taken from the text.

1   I hate going to the dentist's. I d_____ the m_____ when the drill touches my teeth.
2   You've already had a go: now it's my t_____.
3   It was the third time that week that he had brought wild mushrooms home. Oh dear, thought his wife, h_____ we g_____ a_____!
4   You shouldn't be here: please leave a_____ o_____.
5   He had been away for a_____, and everyone had gr_____ t_____ of waiting.
6   This cheese is full of blue veins, but, d_____ its appearance, it is d_____ to eat.

98

7 His face t_____ g_____ when he smelled the bad eggs.

8 People who live in cities have l_____ all c_____ with the countryside.

9 Wild mushroom dishes are a Sunday l_____ sp_____ in many restaurants.

10 A pinch of salt will b_____ o_____ the fl_____ of the soup.

C

Questions for discussion.

1 What do you learn from this story about the Catalan character (or at least the writer's view of it)?

2 If you had to describe Mrs Balaguer to someone else, what could you say about (a) her physical appearance; (b) her character; (c) the success of her marriage?

3 The writer describes the hunt for *bolets* (wild mushrooms) as 'like a religious crusade' and 'madness'. Do you agree? Talk with other people to see if you can find other examples of this kind of activity.

Summer-blue Eyes

GLOSSARY

shows up (line 4): makes obvious.

lines (line 6) and *wrinkles* (line 6): as you get older, the lines on your face break up and turn into wrinkles.

call a spade a spade (line 6): be frank even if it offends someone.

pull yourself together (line 7): regain control of your feelings.

sorry for yourself (line 7–8): full of self-pity.

Damn (line 9): to hell with . . .

Fancy hearing (line 11): imagine hearing. 'Fancy' suggests surprise.

pick me up (line 24): a young man chasing girls is like a hunter. If he is successful, he will catch one, that is, pick one up.

fair game (line 25): the expression comes from hunting; 'fair game' are animals which one is permitted to hunt by law.

turn his oily charm on them (line 26): the word 'oily' suggests that his charm is false, as if it had been oiled to make it come out more smoothly.

tiresome male (line 36–7): irritating. She uses the word 'male' rather than 'man' to imply that the whole male sex behaves in this way.

trying it on (line 37): seeing if he can succeed, get away with it.

He was just being friendly (line 37): the continuous form, 'was being', means that he was behaving in a friendly way at that moment, not that he was necessarily friendly by nature.

Funny, an Arab . . . (line 52): it was odd, peculiar, to see an Arab . . .

green (line 55): innocent; inexperienced.

you cannot afford to cry (line 77): because, if she cries, her face will look even older, more lined, etc.

You look dreadful enough as it is, without . . . (line 77–8): Don't make things even worse by . . .

I saw him on to the coach (line 81): I accompanied him to the coach.

cried my eyes out (line 83): cried bitterly, until I was exhausted.

migraine (line 83): a very bad headache, with vomiting and temporary blindness.

three whole days (line 84): 'whole' emphasises how long she was ill.

whirlwind romance (line 95): that is, very sudden and unexpected.

there was no point in waiting (line 97): it was useless to wait.

thirty years on (line 105): thirty years later.

cannot, for the life of me, remember . . . (line 105–6): really cannot remember at all.

LANGUAGE PRACTICE

A

Replace the words underlined with an expression from the text based on the word(s) given in brackets. Make any necessary grammatical changes.

Example: He suddenly started to laugh (burst).
          He burst out laughing.

1 This is no time for self-pity (sorry).

2 Can you believe it! Juan has left his wife (fancy).

3 I accompanied him to the coach back to London (see).

4 Come on, let's be very honest about it: he's a liar (spade).

5 As the train approached, the children began to wave (nearer).

6 He's in a terrible state: he must try and get back to normal (together).

7 It would be useless to try to wake him up (point).

8 I really cannot remember at all where I put my keys (life).

9 I felt a lovely tingling when he stroked my hair (shiver/spine).

10 With all your problems, it would be foolish to give up your job as well (as it is).

B

Supply the missing words. In some cases, but not all, the first letter of the missing word is given. All these expressions are taken from the text.

1 We met at nine in the morning and were h_____ o_____ h_____ in love by midday.

2 Sarah c_____ her eyes o_____ when she was told she couldn't have a dog.

3 We s_____ the w_____ day together.

4 The trouble with bright lights is that they s_____ _____ every line _____ your face.

5 He spoke to one girl after another, hoping to p_____ one of them_____.

6 Robert and I did not have a w_____ romance: it _____ us ages to _____ up _____ minds to _____ married.

7 Lines g_____ a woman's face c_____. But are they lines or wr_____?

8 I was listening _____ a programme _____ Tunisia _____ the radio the other day.

C

Questions for discussion.

1 If you had to describe Sylvia to someone else, what would you tell them about (a) her physical appearance; (b) her character?

2 She said that they were 'head over heels in love by midday'. Can such things really happen? What if they had got married?

3 We are told very little about her husband, Robert. Discuss with someone what you can find out about him from the story, and then imagine what kind of man, and what kind of husband, he must be.

The Joker

GLOSSARY

to stay in touch (line 7): to keep in contact with each other.

telling people's fortunes (line 10): saying what will happen to them in the future.

posh (line 12): snobbish and expensive.

practical joke (line 24): a trick played on someone, usually with the intention of making him look foolish.

somehow (line 35): that is, we are not sure how he did it.

ran (line 36): continued.

well-to-do (line 43): prosperous.

ended up as (line 49): finally became.

went into business (line 50): a 'business' in this sense could be any kind of enterprise which involves selling goods or services.

followed in his father's footsteps (line 51): entered his father's profession or business.

every bit as (line 56): just as; equally.

ladykiller (line 57): a man who is very attractive to and popular with women; a man who makes conquests of women.

all the time in the world (line 63–4): enough time to do what you want to do without hurrying.

swept Mrs Ground off her feet (line 69–70): was so charming and persuasive that she could not resist him.

wicked country ways (line 70–71): 'wicked' describes someone who does bad things; 'country ways' suggests sexual misbehaviour.

juicy (line 71): full and rich, like a ripe fruit.

by invitation only (line 78): only people who had been invited could attend.

read out (line 80): read aloud.

Ahem! (line 84): a little cough, the noise made when you want to make people pay attention.

gasped (line 94): a gasp is an escape of breath which usually expresses astonishment.

you could have heard a pin drop (line 100): a fixed expression to describe absolute silence; for example: 'It was so quiet that you could have heard a pin drop'.

it's up to you now (line 106): it is your responsibility; you must take over.

screwed-up (line 112): held tightly shut.

cover up (line 119): hide; disguise.

giggle (line 123): childish laughter.

In no time (line 138): in a very short time; soon.

they had been been set up (line 151): a trap had been set for them, and they had fallen into it.

letting the meaning of the words sink in (line 157): allowing people time to realise the real meaning behind the words.

LANGUAGE PRACTICE

A

Replace the words underlined with an expression from the text based on the word(s) given in brackets. Make any necessary grammatical changes.

Example: He <u>suddenly started to laugh</u> (burst).
        He burst out laughing.

1   I've taught you all I can: <u>you are responsible for yourself</u> now (up).

2   John decided to <u>go into the same profession as</u> his father (footsteps).

3 Now that I've retired, I have <u>plenty of leisure</u> to pursue my hobbies (time/world).

4 <u>It was obvious</u> that he was lying (doubt).

5 All the Ground brothers <u>did very well in life</u> (success/lives).

6 Sarah is <u>just</u> as clever as her brother (bit).

7 Now that we have met again after <u>such a long time</u> . . . (years).

8 . . . we must try to <u>maintain contact with each other</u> from now on (touch).

9 Everyone stopped talking: <u>there was not a sound</u> (pin).

10 I didn't recognise her at first. Then <u>I suddenly realised</u> who she was (dawn).

B

Supply the missing words. In most cases, but not all, the first letter(s) of the missing word is (are) given. All these expressions are taken from the text.

1 It's difficult to k_____ a s_____ face when everyone r_____ you is laughing and g_____.

2 He went into the art gallery and t_____ all the pictures u_____ d_____.

3 A pr_____ joker enjoys p_____ people's l_____.

4 When he sneezed and then b_____ his n_____ very loudly, everyone b_____ _____ laughing.

5 You could t_____ _____ the way she behaved that she liked b_____ the _____ of attention.

6 He was s_____ a ladykiller that he just s_____ her _____ her f_____.

7 A palmist can t_____ your f_____ just _____ looking at your hand.

8 He started _____ as a clerk and e_____ up _____ a bank manager.

9 Just because you're in a bad mood, don't t_____ it _____ _____ other people.

10 I thought he was a tramp, but he t_____ _____ to be a duke.

C

Questions for discussion.

1 What can you say about Henry Ground's background? Compare him with his brothers, and say whether you regard him as a 'lazy, good-for-nothing'.

2 What makes people want to play practical jokes? What kind of people become practical jokers, do you think? Are they happy people? Kind? Selfish?

3 Describe to someone else the scene where Henry's will was read out. Do you think that Henry had any reason for playing this last joke on his friends, apart from just having a bit of fun?

If There is Water

Note: Angola is a former Portuguese colony. The story is set in southern Angola, the part worst affected by the civil war.

GLOSSARY

were to spend (line 11): 'were to' gives the idea that it was planned.
which was not always the case (line 35–6): it was not always like this.
setting up (line 38): arranging; organising.
squeezing information out (line 40): like squeezing juice out of a lemon.
what was left (line 44): what had not been destroyed in the war.
escarpment (line 47–8): the steep descent from the plateau to the desert.
leave (line 52): a soldier's rest from duty.
from the front (line 52): from the battle zone.
pot-holes (line 59–60): deep holes in the road.
chattered (line 60): talked endlessly and noisily about unimportant things.
lining the roadside (line 69): standing along both sides of the road.
made more stark (line 70): emphasised; made more noticeable.
milled (line 73): crowded round.

stopped short of saying (line 75): decided not to say what was in his mind.

on the point of (line 86): just about to.

thought better of it (line 87): decided it would be better to say nothing.

had all the makings (line 93): everything needed to cause a disaster.

temper (line 109): feeling of anger.

lurking (line 124): lying in wait ready to attack.

showing her concern (line 130): showing that she was worried about him.

wolfed (line 138); *nibbled* (line 138); *began to chew* (line 139): ways of
   describing eating: *wolfed*: like a wolf, greedily; *nibbled*: like a mouse,
   daintily; *chew*: bite repeatedly. The word suggests effort.

its resemblance to wood (line 139–40): it was like wood.

curse the food (line 141): say that the food was terrible.

all but (line 147): almost; very nearly.

Time we were getting back (line 148–9): we ought to leave now. Note
   the tenses: It *is* time we *were* . . .

had had enough (line 149): was tired of; fed up with.

anxious to (line 150): very much wanted to. 'Anxious' suggests that you
   are worried about the consequences if you do not do what you are
   anxious to do.

in time for dinner (line 156): not too late.

take his mind off (line 160): make himself think of something pleasanter.

stopped Victor in his tracks (line 179): he suffered a shock. It is like
   suddenly being forced to stop when you are moving forward quickly.

difficult to take in (line 181): difficult to realise, to comprehend.

and that, only if . . . (line 182–3): and they would be able to have
   soup only if . . .

little time (line 185–6): almost no time.

a salad of sorts (line 189): a sort of salad, but obviously not a good one.

went straight to his room (line 192): went immediately, without delay.

queer (line 193): unwell, but not knowing exactly what was wrong.

flaking plaster (line 196): small pieces ('flakes') had come away from the
   ceiling.

belly (line 199): a vulgar word for stomach.

halting English (line 215): her speech was full of pauses and hesitations.

A

Replace the words underlined with an expression from the text based on the word(s) given in brackets. Make any necessary grammatical changes.

Example: He <u>suddenly started to laugh</u> (burst).
             He burst out laughing.

1   I was <u>about to tell</u> him to shut up, but . . . (point)
2   . . . <u>decided that it was not a good idea</u> (better).
3   We told him funny stories to <u>keep him from thinking about</u> his illness (mind).
4   Her story was so fantastic that it was difficult to <u>believe it all</u> (take).
5   I <u>am really tired</u> of listening to such rubbish (enough).
6   I'm glad that your children and mine <u>are such good friends</u> (well together).
7   If we are to be there by noon, <u>we must</u> set off before dawn (mean).
8   <u>You really ought to get</u> your hair cut (time/got).
9   How many people have been invited? <u>I believe</u> you are the only one (far/know).
10   Who organised the meeting? Marina <u>arranged it</u> (set).

B

Supply the missing words. In each case, the first letter(s) of the missing word is (are) given. All these expressions are taken from the text.

1   We usually go for a drink after work, but last night we went s_____ h_____ .
2   The news that I had won a million pounds st_____ me in my t_____ .
3   The situation had a_____ the m_____ of a disaster.
4   He was a_____ to g_____ back to the hotel i_____ t_____ for dinner.
5   The girls n_____ their bread, Zé w_____ his d_____ , and Victor c_____ on his as if it were a piece of wood.

6 The hotel was full of soldiers o_____ l_____ from the f_____.

7 He shook her hand, but st_____ sh_____ of kissing her.

8 Because of the war, the transport system had a_____ b_____ collapsed.

9 Domingues sh_____ her c_____ for poor Victor by offering him some water.

10 We left the hotel after lunch and m_____ our w_____ to the town centre.

C

Questions for discussion.

1 If you were asked to describe Domingues to someone else, what could you say about (a) her physical appearance; (b) her background; (c) her character? What kind of a person does she appear, in your opinion, to (a) Marina; (b) Victor?

2 Domingues formed a good impression of Victor when she first met him (see lines 33–6). Do you think she was right about him?

3 This story is set in the post-colonial period. What do you learn from the story about what has changed and what has not changed since independence? Do you think Victor was right to describe it as 'this poor, confused country' (line 198)?